THE SUPER EASY VEGETARIAN SLOW COOKER COOKBOOK

THE SUPER EASY

VEGETARIAN SLOW COOKER

COOKBOOK

115 Easy, Healthy Recipes Ready When You Are

Kristi Arnold

ROCKRIDGE
PRESS

To The Fam. Thanks for the always.

For general information on our other products and services or to obtain technical support, please contact our Customer Care Department within the United States at (866) 744-2665, or outside the United States at (510) 253-0500.

Rockridge Press publishes its books in a variety of electronic and print formats. Some content that appears in print may not be available in electronic books, and vice versa.

TRADEMARKS: Rockridge Press and the Rockridge Press logo are trademarks or registered trademarks of Callisto Media Inc. and/or its affiliates, in the United States and other countries, and may not be used without written permission. All other trademarks are the property of their respective owners. Rockridge Press is not associated with any product or vendor mentioned in this book.

Interior & Cover Designer: Emma Hall
Art Producer: Sue Bischofberger
Editor: Andrea Leptinsky
Production Editor: Matthew Burnett

Photography © 2019 Andrew Purcell. Food styling by Carrie Purcell.
Author photo provided by Maegan Hall Photography.

ISBN: Print 978-1-64152-715-6 | eBook 978-1-64152-716-3

INTRODUCTION

As the founder of VeggieConverter.com and a 20-year vegetarian, when I married Mr. Meaty, I found that having meals together could be a challenge. In fact, in the first few years of our marriage, we often ate separate meals together—mine with lots of vegetables; his with lots of meat.

But then our first little one—Tall Fry—joined us and meals started to get more complicated. And when Small Fry joined the crew, it seemed like we had to make three different meals to satisfy all our dietary needs. I also realized that, even though I thought I led a healthy life and ate a nutritious vegetarian diet, I had A LOT to learn. Every time I thought I'd cut all the junk food from our home and our diets, I'd find something new I needed to nix.

I started tracking our culinary journey, looking for healthy recipes we could all eat as a family so we could enjoy meals together and I wouldn't be forced to cook something different for each person. Our blended-eater family includes one vegetarian(ish), gluten-free mama, one meaty dad, and two undecided kids, so converting traditional recipe favorites into (mostly) vegetarian meals the entire family can enjoy together hasn't always been easy.

The solution has been to focus on maintaining healthy, green living. We eat easy, organic, family-friendly, whole-food meals that are generally wheat-free and meatless, with a couple of optional meat days to satisfy the omnivores. We also eat sourdough bread on occasion.

I really understand the transition from a "normal" diet in America to a healthier lifestyle can be overwhelming. In my case, instead of kicking myself over all the mistakes I might have made in the past or stressing over being perfect now,

I chose to start fresh and cut myself some slack. I suggest you try the same. Start slow, do what you can each day, and accept the fact that you are making progress, one vegetable at a time.

One thing that really helped me put healthy and delicious meals on the table was my slow cooker. It has made our lives easier and given us more time to be together as a family because I can quickly prep the ingredients, add them to the slow cooker, turn it on, and walk away. Hours later, we can come home to a fully cooked dinner.

And, for those of you out there with an Instant Pot or other electric pressure cooker, guess what? All recipes in this book can easily be adapted to cook in your pressure cooker. The method is pretty similar, just faster. Generally, I find that most slow cooker recipes that cook for 8 hours take about 45 minutes on high pressure in the Instant Pot, and slow cooker recipes that take 4 hours on high can take as little as 10 to 15 minutes on high pressure in the pressure cooker.

Either way, you are spending less time in the kitchen and more time keeping your hands free for kid and pet wrangling, or taking care of those chores you never seem to get to. Chop ingredients the night before, plop everything into the slow cooker in the morning, press some buttons, and go on about your merry, scheduled day. Hours later, you'll come home to a healthy, wholesome, and super-tasty home-cooked vegetarian meal for the entire family.

I hope this cookbook helps you incorporate healthy, easy (and cost-saving!) meatless meals into your family's lifestyle—simply and deliciously!

1

SLOW COOKING FOR A BUSY LIFE

My favorite aspect of slow cooking is how easy it is to make healthy food for my family. I can walk away from my kitchen in the morning and still be cooking a delicious meal my whole family will enjoy. How awesome is that?

MAKE IT EASY

Slow cookers are excellent tools for busy people who want to whip up meals on a budget—think of it as your frugal kitchen friend! You can grab whatever is on sale at your grocery store or local market, chop the ingredients, toss them into the cooker, give it all a quick stir, and let the slow cooker work its magic.

MAKE IT FAST . . . YES, *FAST*

One of the best things about the recipes in this book is that the prep times are fast, so the time you spend in the kitchen is minimal. Prepping fresh ingredients can be done the night before and you'll find the time rarely exceeds 10 minutes, or not by much—the rest is completely hands-free.

Even better: If you use frozen, pre-chopped, or canned ingredients, the prep time is next to nothing, because all you're doing is adding them into the slow cooker. Don't be tempted to use overly processed canned soups or commercial cheese food. Don't worry, you won't find any of that here—these recipes are made with whole-food ingredients. My kids even make our pasta from scratch (you don't have to do that; they just enjoy making pasta—it's Zen for them, or something).

Slow Cooking Tips

Try these handy tips for healthy, easy slow cooking:

Add pasta and rice last. If you add pasta or rice to the slow cooker about 15 minutes before the recipe is finished, you will avoid overcooking it.

Chop veggies. Cut them into equal pieces to ensure consistent and even cook times.

Cover the slow cooker. Always cover your slow cooker unless otherwise directed. This will keep the heat concentrated inside and the food will cook more evenly.

Prep ingredients the night before. If you prepare vegetables and fruits before you go to bed, you'll be able to throw them into the slow cooker first thing on cook day.

Use inserts. If a recipe calls for a smaller slow cooker than you have, use an ovenproof insert, like a glass Pyrex dish, which also makes cleanup easier if you are cooking a sticky dessert.

Use the "low" setting. Use the low heat setting on the slow cooker whenever possible, which allows you to cook many recipes for 8 hours.

MAKE IT DELICIOUS!

Some people think becoming a vegetarian means eating the same boring meals night after night but I have never found that to be true. Vegetarian and vegan meals can be exciting and delicious and there are many ways to prepare and spice up your meals so you can have something different every night of the week. Trust me; I know! I once made a different vegetarian dish every day for an entire year and wrote about it on my blog. I never ran out of great things to make—even in December, when I'd already made 334 unique vegetarian meals! I eat things like Cuban Lentil Picadillo (page 135) one night and Asian Lettuce Wraps (page 52) the next and Cashew Chickpeas (page 127) after that. If I'm feeling like something more in the comfort food realm, I go for macaroni and cheese, using the Real Food Mac and Cheese Sauce (page 25), or Lentil Shepherd's Pie (page 142).

The variety of vegetarian ingredients available in grocery stores today is astounding compared to 20 years ago. You don't need to live on grilled cheese and bean burritos every day—and this cookbook is a great place to start.

Variety is the Spice of Life

Sometimes, it pays to make the same meals regularly. If certain veggies are in season or something goes on sale, you might find yourself in a bit of a recipe rut. But to keep things fresh for your family, it's nice to have set meal plans to keep from losing your mind during busy school years and heavy work schedules (obviously speaking for a friend here . . .).

Even if you make certain recipes regularly you can still change them up a bit each time you serve them. That's where toppings come to the rescue. These can be real meal savers for vegetarians and for families like mine that include a mix of vegetarians and meat lovers. Toppings offer a little variety for any meal. Think about adding different toppings to the humble taco, like I do with the Build Your Own Tacos Bar (page 111), or a potato with the Build Your Own Loaded Baked Potatoes (page 112)—it can change the flavors radically and give your family a totally different dining experience. These buffet-style meals serve our family well, as they allow everyone to spice up their meals with their own particular flavor combinations. We consider toppings our dinnertime savior.

Here are a few of our favorite toppings:

- Black sesame seeds
- Chopped nuts
- Curry powder
- Fresh herbs, such as basil, cilantro, lemongrass, rosemary, and thyme
- Garlic powder
- Gochujang (Korean chile paste)
- Malt vinegar
- Mexican hot sauce
- Nutritional yeast (imparts a cheesy flavor)
- Onion powder
- Sesame seeds
- Scallions
- Sriracha
- Taco Seasoning (page 32)

MAKE IT HEALTHY

When eating a vegetarian diet, it is important to get a balanced amount of protein, healthy fats, and carbohydrates. Vegetarian meals often center on a protein base—but don't hyper-focus so much on that one component that you forget about everything else. Protein is important, but so are carbohydrates and healthy fats.

Grains and root vegetables are vegetarian diet staples for a good reason—they're packed with fiber, vitamins, minerals, and antioxidants and they are perfect for the slow cooker. Add green vegetables and a variety of nutrient-rich fruits to the mix, and you'll create a balanced vegetarian diet with the help of your slow cooker.

Easy Protein Sources

You don't need processed fake meats to get the protein you need. You likely already know about beans and lentils, but there are tons of other options. Ingredients with healthy proteins that easily stand in for meat and bring color, vibrancy, and nutrition to your plate include:

- Avocado
- Chickpeas
- Coconut
- Edamame
- Halloumi cheese
- Jackfruit
- Mushrooms
- Quinoa
- Seeds and nuts (I love chia and hemp seeds for smoothies, plus almonds, cashews, and walnuts are great for snacking and adding to recipes.)

MAKE IT EFFICIENT

With a little organization, preparation, and thoughtful storage, making vegetarian meals in the slow cooker can save you precious time in the kitchen—time better spent having fun and enjoying life.

The first thing to do is keep your slow cooker in a place where it's easy to access it. I keep mine on a shelf near, but not on, the kitchen counter. That way it doesn't clutter up my prep space, but it's still within easy reach when I'm ready for it on a busy morning.

I also make sure to keep the slow cooker within the "kitchen prep triangle zone," which is the highly used part of your kitchen specifically designed for its ease of use: the oven, sink, refrigerator, and pantry. They are usually positioned so the person making the food can access all those elements efficiently and easily.

Efficiency, to me, also means using similar ingredients throughout the week and buying whatever is in season. I'll even change my meal plan on the fly while at the grocery store if I find something great on sale.

Another great way to save time is to refrigerate leftovers if you plan to eat them during the week or freeze them to eat within a few months. That means you can cook once and eat three or four times from a single slow cooker meal. For even more efficiency, divide leftovers into single servings and they'll be ready to head with you to work or school. For soups, I often use silicone muffin tins to freeze small portions for future meals. Once frozen, I pop them out and store them in a freezer bag.

Menu Prep

We have found, over the years, that meal planning a few meals a week and winging it for the rest is the most efficient way to operate our family meals (and budget). We usually plan to make three or four slow cooker meals over the weekend. Throughout the week, we eat those meals or use leftover ingredients in related meals. It's a great way to get through a busy week without spending all your time planning or overloading your pantry or refrigerator (or your composter if you can't get through all the food before it spoils, which drives me crazy). For example, we plan for Taco Tuesdays, Salad Wednesdays, and Chickpea Thursdays. The rest of the days are a bit on the fly, or based on that week's leftovers.

Another week might include Black Bean Lentil Chili (page 85), Real Food Mac and Cheese Sauce (page 25), and Build Your Own Loaded Baked Potatoes (page 112) for the three planned meals. The beauty of this plan is that it works together. The chili is great the first day and even better the next. Here's how it would work:

On Monday, we might eat something leftover from the weekend or something quickly prepared from the pantry or refrigerator. On Tuesday, we would make the chili and eat it for dinner. The macaroni and cheese would be for Wednesday night dinner. On Thursday or Friday, we would enjoy an amazing buffet of Loaded Baked Potatoes with assorted toppings, like the chili, cheese sauce, broccoli, or whatever else looks good that we have on hand. And on a leftovers day we can make a chili cheese mac using the leftovers. Brilliant. For maximum efficiency, check your pantry to see what you have before adding something to the shopping list.

A shopping list for that plan would include:

- Bell pepper, green (1)
- Black beans, dried (1 pound)
- Broccoli (1 head)
- Lentils, dried, any color (2 cups)
- Onion, yellow (1)
- Pasta (1 pound)
- Tomatoes, large (4)

Items I probably already have at home include:

- Broth, vegetable
- Butter
- Cheese, shredded
- Chili powder
- Chives, fresh
- Cumin, ground
- Flour, gluten-free
- Garlic
- Hot sauce
- Jalapeño peppers
- Milk
- Mustard, ground
- Pepper, cayenne
- Pepper, black, freshly ground
- Salt
- Sour cream

Ingredients and Shopping Tips

Now, I'm a huge fan of cooking with whole foods and making meals from scratch. However, that doesn't mean you can't take a few shortcuts or prep a few things ahead to save yourself time in the kitchen. You can purchase jars of minced garlic (or chop fresh garlic and freeze it), minced onion, washed greens, ginger paste, curry paste, frozen riced cauliflower, and the like.

Frozen vegetables ideal for slow cooking include hearty varieties such as Brussels sprouts and cauliflower, as well as last-minute drop-in-the-slow-cooker veggies such as corn and peas.

Beans and grains taste amazing when cooked in a slow cooker. Large bags of dried beans are inexpensive compared to canned and they can cook for hours in your slow cooker without any active time in the kitchen—you'll wonder why you haven't tried preparing them this way sooner. If you cook a large double batch of Slow-Cooked Beans (page 15), which yields 12 cups cooked beans, it will cost less than the price of a single can.

But I think one of the most important aspects of slow cooking is flavor. Because you're cooking low and slow, whatever is cooking gains tons of flavor. Taste as soon as your dish is finished cooking and adjust the seasoning with salt, pepper, herbs, and spices, as needed.

Top Pantry and Fridge Ingredients to Stock

Whether you eat vegetarian once a week, once a month, or are making a permanent transition, cooking will be a lot easier if you keep staple ingredients in your pantry and refrigerator, available to make versatile, nutritional meals. Cheese and bread just won't cut it. If you have chickpeas, for example, you can make Falafel (page 96), Chickpea Nuggets (page 129), or Pesto Chickpeas (page 132).

Here are my top 10 favorite ingredients. If you have these, you'll be able to make many of the recipes in this book.

1. Black beans
2. Broccoli
3. Carrots
4. Cashews
5. Chickpeas
6. Lentils
7. Peas
8. Quinoa
9. Rice
10. Tomatoes

SLOW COOKER BAKING DISHES

Baking in the slow cooker can present its own set of challenges. You'll probably need a baking dish to put inside the slow cooker, and there are a few considerations and tips to take into account when it comes to choosing the right one.

CLEANUP. Using a baking dish as an insert for your slow cooker makes cleanup simpler. The slow cooker crock is heavy, bulky, and often too big to put into the dishwasher. Most baking dishes can go right into the dishwasher, so they're a snap to clean. Plus, if you have something else to cook right after your baking is finished, you can do so easily, without having to clean out the pot.

OVEN SAFETY. Choose an oven-safe baking dish, made of oven-safe glass (Pyrex), metal, or ceramic.

SIZE. Check the size of your baking dish BEFORE you load it with ingredients. If the baking dish won't fit into your slow cooker, it's a waste.

SHAPE. This is a personal preference. Do you want your bread to be a rectangle or an oval? Choose a glass loaf pan if you want rectangular bread. Choose a ceramic casserole dish if you want an oval or a circle. As mentioned previously, the main concern is that it fits in your slow cooker.

WATER BATH. The baking dish is important if you need to create a water bath. In recipes like Blueberry-Lemon Bread Pudding (page 155), you will add water to the slow cooker, which creates a steamy environment for your dessert to bake in.

ABOUT THE RECIPES

SIZES. Slow cookers come in several sizes, from the smaller 2-quart, which is great for 1 or 2 people, to larger 4- and 6-quart slow cookers ideal for most family recipes. If you only buy one slow cooker, I suggest a 6-quart size. It'll work for all the recipes in this book and you can always insert a baking dish for recipes that call for something smaller.

PREP TIMES. The average preparation time for most recipes here is about 10 to 15 minutes. Because most recipes in this cookbook start from scratch and use whole foods, you will see a few that require up to 25 minutes and some others that ask you to soak an ingredient overnight or prep something over several days (like Sourdough Starter and Sourdough Bread [page 49]). If you're not an experienced cook, start with the simpler recipes first and, once you get used to how the recipes work, tackle the slightly more involved ones.

COOKING TIMES. Most recipes cook for about 8 hours on low; however, you'll see several sides and desserts that take less time.

INGREDIENTS. Most recipes use no more than five major ingredients. Some recipes have significantly more, especially if you start counting spices in some of the recipes featuring global flavors. But, when you are cooking with vegetable proteins, spice is where you'll get most of your flavor.

DIETARY RESTRICTIONS. For those with dietary restrictions, I've included labels with each recipe to let the reader know if they are gluten-free, nightshade-free, nut-free, soy-free, or vegan.

- **Gluten-free.** Those with celiac disease cannot eat gluten and there is a wide group of people sensitive to gluten and who want to avoid it. If this is a concern for you, always check package ingredients for gluten-free labeling and to ensure foods, especially oats, were processed in a completely gluten-free facility.

- **Nightshade-free.** Tomatoes, eggplants, peppers, and potatoes are the main vegetables that fall under the nightshade category and contain solanine, a chemical thought to contribute to inflammation.

- **Nut-free.** Many people are allergic to one or more nuts.

- **Soy-free.** Some people avoid soy because it contains isoflavones, which act like estrogen in the body.

- **Vegan.** These recipes have no animal products, including meat, dairy, eggs, or honey.

TIPS. Throughout the recipes I've included tips to make cooking easier or to change up the flavor if you decide to enjoy the dish more than once.

Basmati Rice Breakfast Cereal, page 24

2

STAPLES

VEGETABLE SCRAP BROTH *Makes 2 quarts*

Whenever you cut up vegetables for a meal, save those scraps! You can keep them in the refrigerator or freeze them until you are ready to make this healthy vegetable broth. This is a must-have item for your pantry—you can use it as a base for soups and stews or for dishes like Cauliflower "Fried" Rice (page 19) and Massaman Curry (page 88)—and it's inexpensive and really easy to make. The broth should be cooked in the slow cooker for at least 12 hours. I usually cook my broth for 24 hours, which deepens the flavors.

2 cups loosely packed vegetable trimmings, such as onion skins and ends, carrot peelings, zucchini ends, and herb stems

1 tablespoon apple cider vinegar

1½ teaspoons whole black peppercorns

1 bay leaf

2 quarts water

GLUTEN-FREE
NIGHTSHADE-FREE
NUT-FREE
SOY-FREE
VEGAN

PREP TIME
10 minutes
COOK TIME
12 to 24 hours
TOTAL TIME
12 to 24 hours

1. In a 4-quart slow cooker, mix together the vegetable trimmings, vinegar, peppercorns, bay leaf, and water.

2. Cover the slow cooker and cook on low heat for 12 to 24 hours.

3. Place a fine-mesh sieve over a large bowl.

4. When the slow cooker pot is cool enough to handle, strain the broth through the sieve and discard any solids. Pour the broth into 2 one-quart containers with lids.

5. The broth can be refrigerated for up to 5 days or frozen for up to 6 months.

Per Serving (1 cup): Calories: 16; Total Fat: 0g; Sodium: 32g; Sugars: 2g; Carbohydrates: 4g; Fiber: 0g; Protein: 0g

Ingredient Tip: I collect the vegetable trimmings in a freezer bag (avoiding certain veggies, such as broccoli and Brussels sprouts, that may taint the delicate flavor of the broth). Once the bag gets full or I'm ready for a new batch of broth, I add the scraps to whatever vegetables I have on hand and get practically free vegetable broth.

Variation Tip: Make this a mushroom broth by replacing the vegetable scraps with 2 ounces dried mushrooms.

SLOW-COOKED BEANS *Makes 6 cups*

On the weekend, cook up a batch of beans and you'll have meals all week. Beans are inexpensive and dried beans can be stored in your pantry indefinitely. You can use these cooked beans for Black Bean Soup (page 61) or a Build Your Own Tacos Bar (page 111).

2 cups dried beans, such as black beans, pinto beans, or kidney beans

8 cups water, divided

2 teaspoons salt

GLUTEN-FREE
NIGHTSHADE-FREE
NUT-FREE
SOY-FREE
VEGAN

PREP TIME
10 hours

COOK TIME
8 hours

TOTAL TIME
18 hours

1. Place the beans in a large bowl, cover them with about 4 cups of the water, and soak overnight or for up to 10 hours.

2. Drain the beans and rinse them thoroughly. Transfer the beans to a 6-quart slow cooker, stir in the salt, and add the remaining 4 cups of water.

3. Cover the slow cooker and cook on low heat for 8 hours, or until the beans are tender but not mushy.

4. The beans can be refrigerated in an airtight container for up to 5 days or frozen for up to 6 months. Let the beans come to room temperature before using.

Per Serving (1 cup): Calories: 219; Total Fat: 1g; Sodium: 775mg; Sugars: 0g; Carbohydrates: 40g; Fiber: 10g; Protein: 14g

SLOW-COOKED LENTILS *Makes 4 cups*

Lentils are a staple for vegetarians across the world, and they're especially prominent in Indian and Mediterranean cuisines. This recipe is a simple guide for preparing lentils as a base protein, and you can use the cooked lentils in many recipes. Try using cooked green, brown, or French lentils in the Cuban Lentil Picadillo (page 135) or the Lentil Sloppy Joes (page 142). Red, orange, and yellow lentils tend to get mushy and are better for sauces, soups, and stews.

1 cup dried green, brown, or French lentils

4 cups water

½ teaspoon salt

1. Place the lentils in a colander and rinse them with water for about 30 seconds. Transfer the lentils to a 4-quart slow cooker and add the water. Add the salt and stir to combine.

2. Cover the slow cooker and cook for 4 hours on low heat, or until the lentils are tender but not mushy.

3. Drain any excess water from the lentils, if needed.

4. The lentils can be refrigerated in an airtight container for up to 5 days or frozen for up to 6 months. Let the lentils come to room temperature before using.

Per Serving (1 cup): Calories: 169; Total Fat: 1g; Sodium: 294mg; Sugars: 1g; Carbohydrates: 29g; Fiber: 15g; Protein: 12g

GLUTEN-FREE
NIGHTSHADE-FREE
NUT-FREE
SOY-FREE
VEGAN

PREP TIME
10 minutes

COOK TIME
4 hours

TOTAL TIME
4 hours, 10 minutes

Ingredient Tip: Although you shouldn't add acidic ingredients like lemon juice or vinegar to lentils as they cook, you can add other seasonings or flavor enhancers, such as minced garlic, chopped shallot, or freshly ground black pepper. For even more flavor, use vegetable broth instead of water.

RICE *Makes 6 cups*

Rice is great to serve alongside almost any meal and is often an integral part of a vegetarian feast. Perfectly cooked, tender rice can be made in your slow cooker in just a couple hours.

2 cups medium- or short-grain white rice

4 cups water

Pinch salt (optional)

1. Place the rice in a fine-mesh colander and rinse with water until the runoff is clear.

2. Transfer the rice to a 4-quart slow cooker and stir in the water and salt (if using).

3. Cover the slow cooker and cook on low heat for 2 to 2½ hours, or until the rice is tender.

4. Fluff the rice with a fork and serve immediately. To store, let the rice cool to room temperature and refrigerate in an airtight container for up to 5 days or freeze for up to 6 months.

Per Serving (1 cup): Calories: 234; Total Fat: 0g; Sodium: 1mg; Sugars: 0g; Carbohydrates: 52g; Fiber: 0g; Protein: 4g

Sushi Rice Per Serving (1 cup): Calories: 290; Total Fat: 3g; Sodium: 391mg; Sugars: 8g; Carbohydrates: 58g; Fiber: 1g; Protein: 4g

Mexican Rice Per Serving (1 cup): Calories: 260; Total Fat: 0g; Sodium: 426mg; Sugars: 2g; Carbohydrates: 57g; Fiber: 0g; Protein: 5g

GLUTEN-FREE
NIGHTSHADE-FREE
NUT-FREE
SOY-FREE
VEGAN

PREP TIME
5 minutes

COOK TIME
2 to 2½ hours

TOTAL TIME
2 to 2 hours, 35 minutes

Variation Tip: For a sushi rice variation, in a saucepan over medium heat, stir together ½ cup rice vinegar, ¼ cup sugar, 1 tablespoon olive oil, and 1 teaspoon salt, stirring until the sugar dissolves. Let cool and mix with the cooked rice.

For a Mexican rice variation, replace the water in the rice recipe with Vegetable Scrap Broth (page 14). In a small bowl, stir together 2 tablespoons Taco Seasoning (page 32), 2 tablespoons tomato paste, and 1 tablespoon freshly squeezed lime juice until blended and add to the slow cooker with the rice in step 2. Cook as directed.

QUINOA-BROWN RICE BLEND *Makes about 5 cups*

Adding quinoa to your rice is a great way to add protein and nutrients to your meals. And it's super tasty, too.

1½ cups brown rice

2 cups Vegetable Scrap Broth (page 14) or store-bought broth

1 cup quinoa

1 teaspoon salt

3 cups water

GLUTEN-FREE
NIGHTSHADE-FREE
NUT-FREE
SOY-FREE
VEGAN

PREP TIME
5 minutes

COOK TIME
2½ to 3 hours

TOTAL TIME
2½ to 3 hours, 5 minutes

1. In a fine-mesh colander, rinse the brown rice and quinoa until the runoff is clear. Transfer the rice and quinoa to a 4-quart slow cooker.

2. Stir in the salt, vegetable broth, and water.

3. Cover the slow cooker and cook on low heat for 2½ to 3 hours, or until the rice and quinoa are tender.

4. Fluff the rice and quinoa with a fork and serve immediately. To store, let it cool to room temperature and refrigerate in an airtight container for up to 5 days or freeze for up to 6 months.

Per Serving (½ cup): Calories: 169; Total Fat: 2g; Sodium: 8mg; Sugars: 1g; Carbohydrates: 34g; Fiber: 2g; Protein: 5g

CAULIFLOWER "FRIED" RICE

Makes about 6 cups

Cauliflower rice is an excellent, nutrient-packed, low-carb, and grain-free way to enjoy curries and other stew-like meals with a base other than rice or quinoa. This version is a bit like fried rice. If you want a more neutral base, cook it without the eggs, peas, cilantro, scallion, and coconut aminos. For the garlic and ginger, to save a little prep time, buy this already mixed in a tube or in separate tubes in the produce section of your grocery store.

2 heads cauliflower, cut into florets

½ cup Vegetable Scrap Broth (page 14) or store-bought broth

1 tablespoon minced garlic

1 tablespoon ginger paste

2 large eggs, beaten

1 cup frozen peas

¼ cup diced scallion

¼ cup chopped fresh cilantro (optional)

2 tablespoons coconut aminos or soy sauce

GLUTEN-FREE
NIGHTSHADE-FREE
NUT-FREE
SOY-FREE

PREP TIME
15 minutes

COOK TIME
4 hours, 30 minutes

TOTAL TIME
5 hours

1. In a food processor, pulse the cauliflower florets into fine crumbs. Transfer the cauliflower to a 6-quart slow cooker and stir in the vegetable broth, garlic, and ginger paste.

2. Cover the slow cooker and cook on low heat for 3 to 4 hours until the cauliflower is tender.

3. Add the beaten eggs and frozen peas to the slow cooker. Re-cover the cooker and cook for 10 minutes more, until the peas are heated through. Stir in the scallion and cilantro (if using) and drizzle with the coconut aminos.

4. The cauliflower rice can be refrigerated in an airtight container for up to 5 days or frozen for up to 6 months.

Per Serving (1 cup): Calories: 100; Total Fat: 2g; Sodium: 402mg; Sugars: 7g; Carbohydrates: 16g; Fiber: 7g; Protein: 8g

YOGURT *Makes 5 cups*

Making yogurt can be a bit time-consuming, but it's super simple once you get the hang of it and homemade yogurt tastes so much better than the kind you buy. My kids absolutely love the flavor without any added sugar. We usually freeze about half the yogurt in ¼-cup portions, to have around for breakfast smoothies or other recipes.

½ gallon whole milk

½ cup plain whole-milk yogurt

2 tablespoons vanilla extract (optional)

GLUTEN-FREE
NIGHTSHADE-FREE
NUT-FREE
SOY-FREE

PREP TIME
30 minutes
COOK TIME
16 to 18 hours
TOTAL TIME
18 to 20 hours

Variation Tip: Use the yogurt to make raita, tzatziki, ranch dressing, or blue cheese dressing.

1. Pour the milk into a 4-quart or larger slow cooker, cover the cooker, and cook on low heat for 2½ hours.

2. Unplug the slow cooker, keep it covered, and let sit for 3 hours.

3. Whisk in the yogurt and vanilla (if using). Re-cover the cooker and wrap it completely with a kitchen towel. Let sit for 8 hours, or overnight.

4. In the morning, you'll have yogurt. If you like thicker yogurt, line a strainer with coffee filters, or use a nut milk or yogurt straining bag, and place it over a bowl. Ladle the yogurt into the strainer and place the bowl in the refrigerator for several hours.

5. Transfer the yogurt from the strainer into a bowl and whisk until smooth. Save the whey (drained liquid) for making smoothies, as a liquid substitute in baking, or as a broth substitute in creamy soups.

6. The yogurt can be refrigerated in an airtight container for up to 5 days or put into silicone muffin tins and frozen. Once frozen, remove the frozen yogurt from the muffin tin and keep frozen in freezer bags for up to 6 months.

Per Serving (1 cup): Calories: 249; Total Fat: 14g; Sodium: 167mg; Sugars: 16g; Carbohydrates: 19g; Fiber: 0g; Protein: 13g

DAIRY-FREE MILK *Serves 4*

Nut milks are universal. They are all made the same way and require two things: nuts and water. In my opinion, to keep my sanity, they require four things: nuts, water, a blender, and a nut milk bag! The rest is just about figuring out what ratio you prefer.

2 cups nuts of choice   2 cups water

1. Place the nuts and water into a blender. Blend for about 5 minutes, depending on the power of your blender, until the mixture is almost smooth.

2. Place a nut milk bag over a bowl or a pitcher. Pour the nut mixture into the bag and let the mixture strain into the bowl for at least 30 minutes.

3. Using your hands, squeeze the nut milk bag to get out the remaining liquid.

4. The nut milk can be refrigerated for up to 5 days or frozen for up to 6 months.

Per Serving (1 cup, almonds): Calories: 40; Total Fat: 4g; Sodium: 40mg; Sugars: 0g; Carbohydrates: 2g; Fiber: 1g; Protein: 1g

GLUTEN-FREE
NIGHTSHADE-FREE
SOY-FREE
VEGAN

PREP TIME
30 minutes

TOTAL TIME
30 minutes

Variation Tip: Don't throw away the nut pulp. Use it in smoothies or add it to muffin recipes for extra fiber.

OVERNIGHT OATMEAL *Serves 4*

Oatmeal is so tasty on a cold morning and this slow cooker version can be started the night before, allowing you to wake up to a hearty, warm breakfast. Add your favorite toppings, like dried cranberries or apricots, fresh fruit, or nuts such as walnuts or pecans. Chocolate chips are pretty delicious as well.

1 cup old-fashioned rolled oats

3 cups water

¼ cup heavy (whipping) cream

¼ cup packed light brown sugar

GLUTEN-FREE
NIGHTSHADE-FREE
NUT-FREE
SOY-FREE

PREP TIME
5 minutes

COOK TIME
8 hours

TOTAL TIME
8 hours, 5 minutes

1. In a 2-quart slow cooker, stir together the oats and water.

2. Cover the slow cooker and cook on low heat for 8 hours.

3. Add the heavy cream and brown sugar and stir until combined. Serve immediately with the toppings of your choice.

4. Leftover oatmeal can be refrigerated in an airtight container for up to 5 days.

Per Serving: Calories: 161; Total Fat: 7g; Sodium: 9mg; Sugars: 9g; Carbohydrates: 23g; Fiber: 2g; Protein: 3g

BUCKWHEAT GROATS *Serves 4*

Buckwheat groats, the hulled gluten-free kernel of the buckwheat grain, can be cooked like oatmeal and are a heartier version of that breakfast staple. Like oatmeal, these groats are wonderful topped with a variety of fruit, nuts, or seeds.

1 cup buckwheat groats
2 cups milk
2 cups water

GLUTEN-FREE
NIGHTSHADE-FREE
NUT-FREE
SOY-FREE

PREP TIME
5 minutes

COOK TIME
6 to 8 hours

TOTAL TIME
6 to 8 hours, 5 minutes

1. In a 4-quart slow cooker, stir together the buckwheat groats, milk, and water.

2. Cover the slow cooker and cook on low heat for 6 to 8 hours, or until the grains are tender but not mushy.

3. Add any toppings you like and serve immediately.

4. Leftover groats can be refrigerated in an airtight container for up to 5 days.

Per Serving: Calories: 113; Total Fat: 3g; Sodium: 59mg; Sugars: 6g; Carbohydrates: 17g; Fiber: 2g; Protein: 6g

BASMATI RICE BREAKFAST CEREAL *Serves 12*

This is the perfect breakfast, especially when paired with coffee sweetened with Pumpkin Spice Latte Syrup (page 36). I love the rich nuttiness of brown basmati rice combined with the creaminess of coconut milk, which makes this morning meal nicely filling. If you don't like coconut milk, use water instead—the recipe will still taste really good.

1½ cups brown basmati rice, rinsed well

3½ cups coconut milk or water

2 extra cups coconut milk, if desired, for additional creaminess

½ cup coarsely chopped walnuts or almonds, toasted

½ cup currants or raisins

1½ cinnamon sticks

2 green cardamom pods

3 tablespoons flaked coconut, toasted

½ teaspoon freshly grated nutmeg

Maple syrup, for drizzling

GLUTEN-FREE
NIGHTSHADE-FREE
SOY-FREE
VEGAN

PREP TIME
5 minutes

COOK TIME
2½ to 3 hours

TOTAL TIME
2½ to 3 hours, 5 minutes

1. In a slow cooker, combine the rice, coconut milk, walnuts, currants, cinnamon sticks, cardamom, coconut, and nutmeg. Stir to mix.

2. Cover the slow cooker and cook on low heat for 2½ to 3 hours, or until the rice is tender.

3. Fluff the rice with a fork. Remove and discard the cardamom and cinnamon sticks. Spoon the rice into bowls and drizzle with maple syrup.

4. Leftovers can be refrigerated in an airtight container for up to 5 days.

Per Serving: Calories: 235; Total Fat: 14g; Sodium: 8mg; Sugars: 5g; Carbohydrates: 26g; Fiber: 2g; Protein: 4g

REAL FOOD MAC AND CHEESE SAUCE *Serves 4*

When I was a kid, I ate the powdered mac and cheese sauce—and I loved it. However, after I had my kids, I tried it again and it was really bad—even the organic stuff was intolerable. My kids don't care for the powdered stuff either, so now I make this delicious creamy cheese sauce instead. If you're in a hurry, you can also make this quickly in a saucepan on the stovetop.

1 tablespoon olive oil

2 tablespoons butter

1 tablespoon gluten-free flour

1 heaping cup shredded Cheddar cheese or cheese blend of choice

4 ounces cream cheese, cubed

1 cup milk

1 teaspoon minced garlic

½ teaspoon dry mustard

Salt (optional)

GLUTEN-FREE
NIGHTSHADE-FREE
NUT-FREE
SOY-FREE

PREP TIME
10 minutes

COOK TIME
3 hours

TOTAL TIME
3 hours, 10 minutes

1. Pour the olive oil into a 4-quart slow cooker and swirl it around to coat.

2. In a saucepan over medium heat, melt the butter. Add the flour and bring it to a simmer, stirring frequently. Cook for about 5 minutes.

3. Add the cream cheese, Cheddar cheese, milk, garlic, and mustard and season with salt (if using). Stir until combined. Transfer the mixture to the slow cooker.

4. Cover the slow cooker and cook on low heat for 3 hours, stirring a few times during cooking.

5. Serve over noodles, rice, quinoa, baked potatoes, broccoli, or anything you want to taste cheesy.

6. The sauce can be refrigerated in an airtight container for up to 5 days or frozen for up to 6 months.

Per Serving: Calories: 335; Total Fat: 30g; Sodium: 330mg; Sugars: 3g; Carbohydrates: 6g; Fiber: 0g; Protein: 12g

ENGLISH BROWN SAUCE *Makes 2 quarts*

My family and I found ourselves asking why we don't have brown sauce in the United States after a recent visit to England. We figured if we could make ketchup, we could probably swing brown sauce, too. I think we did a great job. This sweet-savory sauce is wonderful poured over dishes like the Lentil Loaf with Balsamic Glaze (page 138). For this recipe, I use whole spices because they impart the best flavor. You can find tamarind paste in the international section of your grocery store or at Asian markets. Enjoy the literal fruits of your labor.

2 cups apple
cider vinegar

1 cup white vinegar

8 ounces tomato paste

4 apples, peeled, cored,
and chopped

3 small red
onions, chopped

1 garlic clove, minced

1¼ cups tamarind paste

1 cup freshly squeezed
orange juice

1 cup apple juice

¼ cup dates, pitted

¼ cup prunes

3 tablespoons molasses

⅔ cup water

¾ teaspoon whole
allspice

½ teaspoon whole cloves

½ teaspoon whole black
peppercorns

½ teaspoon
mustard seeds

1 teaspoon coarse salt

½ teaspoon
onion powder

½ teaspoon ground
cardamom

½ teaspoon ground
cinnamon

GLUTEN-FREE
NUT-FREE
SOY-FREE
VEGAN

PREP TIME
15 minutes

COOK TIME
4 hours

TOTAL TIME
4 hours

1. In a 4-quart slow cooker, stir together the cider vinegar, white vinegar, tomato paste, apples, red onions, garlic, tamarind paste, orange juice, apple juice, dates, prunes, molasses, and water.

2. In a spice grinder or clean coffee grinder, grind the allspice, cloves, peppercorns, mustard seeds, and salt into a powder. Add the spice mixture to the slow cooker along with the onion powder, cardamom, and cinnamon and stir to combine.

3. Cover the slow cooker and cook on low heat for 4 hours.

Continued

4. Using an immersion blender, purée the sauce until smooth. Or transfer to a standard blender, working in batches if needed, and blend until smooth.

5. Use immediately or let it cool to room temperature and transfer the sauce to an airtight container. Refrigerate for up to 1 week or freeze for up to 6 months.

Per Serving (½ cup): Calories: 116; Total Fat: 0g; Sodium: 142mg; Sugars: 21g; Carbohydrates: 28g; Fiber: 3g; Protein: 2g

MUSHROOM GRAVY *Makes about 4 cups*

Mushroom Gravy could be considered a vegetarian staple, and it's called for in the Lentil Loaf with Balsamic Glaze (page 138). It's also great with the Spicy Rice Balls (page 117), Herbed Mashed Potatoes (page 57), and as a vegetarian alternative to traditional turkey gravy at Thanksgiving.

12 tablespoons (1½ sticks) butter, divided

1 onion, chopped

¼ cup gluten-free flour

2 cups mushroom broth (see Vegetable Scrap Broth, page 14, Variation Tip)

1 pound portobello mushrooms, trimmed and sliced

½ teaspoon salt

¼ teaspoon freshly ground black pepper

GLUTEN-FREE
NIGHTSHADE-FREE
NUT-FREE
SOY-FREE

PREP TIME
25 minutes

COOK TIME
5 hours

TOTAL TIME
5 hours, 25 minutes

1. In a skillet over medium-low heat, melt 4 tablespoons of butter. Add the onion and cook for 15 to 20 minutes, stirring frequently, until the onion is caramelized.

2. Add the remaining 8 tablespoons (1 stick) of butter and the flour and whisk into a paste. Gradually add the mushroom broth, whisking to combine. Transfer the mixture to a 6-quart slow cooker and stir in the mushrooms, salt, and pepper.

3. Cover the slow cooker and cook on low heat for 5 hours.

4. Use immediately or let it cool to room temperature and transfer the gravy to an airtight container. Refrigerate for up to 5 days or freeze for up to 6 months.

Per Serving (½ cup): Calories: 191; Total Fat: 18g; Sodium: 276mg; Sugars: 2g; Carbohydrates: 7g; Fiber: 1g; Protein: 3g

HOMEMADE KETCHUP
Makes about 3 cups

My kids are crazy for the flavor of this Homemade Ketchup (okay, I love it, too!). What's great about it is you can flavor it however you like. Want more spice? Add cayenne pepper. Like a little tang? Throw in a little more vinegar. When I make a large batch, I freeze it in ¼-cup portions and thaw them later in the refrigerator as needed.

12 ounces tomato paste

¼ cup honey

2 tablespoons apple cider vinegar

2 teaspoons kosher salt

2 teaspoons garlic powder

½ teaspoon onion powder

1 cup water

GLUTEN-FREE

NUT-FREE

SOY-FREE

PREP TIME
10 minutes

COOK TIME
4 hours

TOTAL TIME
4 hours, 10 minutes

1. In a 2-quart slow cooker, stir together the tomato paste, honey, vinegar, salt, garlic powder, onion powder, and water.

2. Cover the slow cooker and cook on low heat for 4 hours.

3. Transfer the ketchup to clean, empty ketchup bottles or picnic squirt bottles.

4. The ketchup can be refrigerated for up to 1 week or frozen for up to 6 months.

Per Serving (2 tablespoons): Calories: 24; Total Fat: 0g; Sodium: 208mg; Sugars: 5g; Carbohydrates: 6g; Fiber: 1g; Protein: 1g

ENCHILADA SAUCE *Makes 2 cups*

This sauce is incredible. Once my family tasted it, there were no more store-bought cans of enchilada sauce for us. I got the idea for this recipe on a whim after I created our homemade Taco Seasoning (page 32), which I thought might taste great in a sauce. It turned out even better than I could have hoped. Try it on the Enchiladas Nopalitos (page 108).

2 tablespoons avocado oil

2 tablespoons arrowroot powder

6 ounces tomato paste

3 tablespoons Taco Seasoning (page 32)

2 cups water

GLUTEN-FREE
NUT-FREE
SOY-FREE
VEGAN

PREP TIME
10 minutes

COOK TIME
4 hours

TOTAL TIME
4 hours, 10 minutes

1. In a 2-quart slow cooker, stir together the avocado oil, arrowroot powder, tomato paste, taco seasoning, and water.

2. Cover the slow cooker and cook on low heat for 4 hours.

3. Use immediately or let it cool to room temperature and transfer to an airtight container. Refrigerate for up to 5 days or freeze for up to 6 months.

Per Serving (¼ cup): Calories: 58; Total Fat: 4g; Sodium: 173mg; Sugars: 3g; Carbohydrates: 6g; Fiber: 1g; Protein: 1g

TACO SEASONING   *Makes 3 cups*

This Taco Seasoning tastes even better than those packaged versions you can buy at the store. The best part is knowing exactly what ingredients are in the mixture. Use this to make Mexican rice (see Rice, page 17, Variation Tip), Black Bean Soup (page 61), or Mushroom and Pepper Fajitas (page 101).

1 cup dried minced onion

¾ cup chili powder

½ cup ground cumin

¼ cup arrowroot powder or cornstarch

3 tablespoons dried oregano, crushed

2½ tablespoons red pepper flakes

4 teaspoons salt

1 teaspoon garlic powder

GLUTEN-FREE
NUT-FREE
SOY-FREE
VEGAN

PREP TIME
5 minutes

TOTAL TIME
5 minutes

In an airtight container, combine the minced onion, chili powder, cumin, arrowroot powder, oregano, red pepper flakes, salt, and garlic powder. Seal the lid and shake the container until the ingredients are combined. Store at room temperature for up to 6 months.

Per Serving (1 tablespoon): Calories: 18; Total Fat: 1g; Sodium: 216mg; Sugars: 1g; Carbohydrates: 3g; Fiber: 1g; Protein: 1g

ITALIAN SEASONING *Makes 3 cups*

The herbs in this seasoning go so well together and really enhance dishes like Lentil Lasagna (page 140) and White Pizza Dip (page 45). Plus, if you make the seasoning yourself, you won't have to buy pricey pre-mixed herbs.

¾ cup dried oregano

½ cup garlic powder

½ cup dried marjoram

½ cup dried thyme

¼ cup dried basil

¼ cup dried rosemary

¼ cup dried sage

GLUTEN-FREE

NUT-FREE

SOY-FREE

VEGAN

PREP TIME
5 minutes

TOTAL TIME
5 minutes

In an airtight container, combine the oregano, garlic, marjoram, thyme, basil, rosemary, and sage. Seal the lid and shake the container until the ingredients are combined. Store at room temperature for up to 6 months.

Per Serving (1 tablespoon): Calories: 12; Total Fat: 0g; Sodium: 1mg; Sugars: 0g; Carbohydrates: 3g; Fiber: 1g; Protein: 1g

BERBERE SEASONING *Makes 3 cups*

Berbere is an Ethiopian spice mix that includes chili peppers, garlic, ginger, and fenugreek. It's used in Chickpea Doro Wat Stew (page 79). You can also use it to spice up Slow Cooked Lentils (page 16) or add it to cheese sauce to add a new kick to your Real Food Mac and Cheese Sauce (page 25).

2 cups chili powder

1 cup paprika

¼ cup cayenne pepper

1 tablespoon onion powder

1 tablespoon ground ginger

1 tablespoon ground cumin

1 tablespoon ground coriander

1 tablespoon ground cardamom

1 tablespoon ground fenugreek

2 teaspoons garlic powder

2 teaspoons ground cinnamon

2 teaspoons ground allspice

2 teaspoons ground cloves

1 teaspoon ground nutmeg

GLUTEN-FREE
NUT-FREE
SOY-FREE
VEGAN

PREP TIME
5 minutes

TOTAL TIME
5 minutes

In an airtight container, combine the chili powder, paprika, cayenne, onion powder, ginger, cumin, coriander, cardamom, fenugreek, garlic powder, cinnamon, allspice, cloves, and nutmeg. Seal the lid and shake the container until the ingredients are combined. Store at room temperature for up to 6 months.

Per Serving (1 tablespoon): Calories: 28; Total Fat: 1g; Sodium: 54mg; Sugars: 1g; Carbohydrates: 5g; Fiber: 3g; Protein: 1g

PUMPKIN PIE SPICE

Makes 2 cups

Pumpkin Pie Spice is one of the true heralds of fall flavor. The warming, cozy flavors will make you want to stay by the fire and snuggle up with a good book. Try it out in Pumpkin Custard Cups (page 164).

1 cup ground cinnamon
½ cup ground ginger
¼ cup ground cloves

2 tablespoons ground nutmeg
1 tablespoon ground allspice

In an airtight container, combine the cinnamon, ginger, cloves, nutmeg, and allspice. Seal the lid and shake the container until the ingredients are combined. Store at room temperature for up to 6 months.

Per Serving (1 tablespoon): Calories: 19; Total Fat: 1g; Sodium: 3mg; Sugars: 0g; Carbohydrates: 5g; Fiber: 2g; Protein: 0g

GLUTEN-FREE
NIGHTSHADE-FREE
NUT-FREE
SOY-FREE
VEGAN

PREP TIME
5 minutes

TOTAL TIME
5 minutes

PUMPKIN SPICE LATTE SYRUP *Serves 8*

Mmm . . . Pumpkin Spice Latte Syrup is not just for coffee; it's also fantastic drizzled over ice cream (try it with coconut milk ice cream). Sometimes my lucky little children get coconut milk push pops, with this pumpkin spice syrup swirled in, placed in their lunch boxes in fall. This recipe is incredibly simple to make, and I keep the syrup on hand to pour into my coffee whenever I like.

1½ cups maple syrup
½ cup pumpkin purée
8 cinnamon sticks
2 teaspoons ground nutmeg
1 tablespoon vanilla extract

1 teaspoon ground cloves
1 teaspoon ground ginger
3 cups water

GLUTEN-FREE
NIGHTSHADE-FREE
NUT-FREE
SOY-FREE
VEGAN

PREP TIME
5 minutes
COOK TIME
8 to 10 hours on low /
4 to 6 hours on high
TOTAL TIME
4 to 10 hours, 5 minutes

1. In a 2- or 4-quart slow cooker, stir together the maple syrup, pumpkin, cinnamon sticks, nutmeg, vanilla, cloves, ginger, and water.

2. Cover the slow cooker and cook on low heat for 8 hours.

3. Remove and discard the cinnamon sticks and pour the mixture into a glass jar or other container with a lid.

4. Add about 1 tablespoon of the syrup to a cup of coffee with cream for a pumpkin spice latte, or drizzle over ice cream.

5. The syrup can be refrigerated for up to 2 weeks. You can also pour the syrup into an ice cube tray, freeze it, transfer the cubes to a freezer bag, and store frozen for up to 6 months.

Per Serving: Calories: 169; Total Fat: 0g; Sodium: 7mg; Sugars: 36g; Carbohydrates: 42g; Fiber: 1g; Protein: 0g

CHAI SYRUP *Serves 12*

I love the combination of spices in chai, but making it fresh each time can be a pain. Keep this syrup on hand and you can have a chai latte whenever you like. I get black cardamom pods from my local Indian grocer but you can order them online from Amazon as well.

10 black tea bags, or 2½ cups loose tea

7 cinnamon sticks

7 whole cloves

7 whole allspice berries

7 black cardamom pods

1 (½-inch) piece crystalized ginger

8 cups water

GLUTEN-FREE
NIGHTSHADE-FREE
NUT-FREE
SOY-FREE
VEGAN

PREP TIME
30 minutes

COOK TIME
8 hours

TOTAL TIME
8 hours, 30 minutes

1. In a 4-quart slow cooker, stir together the tea, cinnamon sticks, cloves, allspice, cardamom pods, ginger, and water.

2. Cover the slow cooker and cook on low heat for 8 hours or overnight.

3. If using loose tea, strain the mixture through a nut milk bag once cool enough to handle. If using tea bags, remove them.

4. Strain out the spices and pour the mixture into a glass jar or other airtight container. To use, combine equal parts chai syrup with your milk of choice and heat.

5. The chai syrup can be refrigerated for up to 2 weeks. You can also pour the syrup into an ice cube tray, freeze it, transfer the cubes to a freezer bag, and store frozen for up to 6 months.

Per Serving (2 tablespoons): Calories: 0; Total Fat: 0g; Sodium: 10mg; Sugars: 0g; Carbohydrates: 0g; Fiber: 0g; Protein: 0g

Samosa Bites, page 43

3

SNACKS, DIPS, AND SIDES

APPLESAUCE *Makes 2 quarts*

If you have children under 20 years old, you need applesauce to survive. Buying the jarred stuff is convenient, sure, but making your own is easy and so delicious! For this recipe, I recommend using organic apples to avoid any pesticide residue that is hard to wash off. For apple varieties, I usually use Gala or Fuji apples, but you can use whichever varieties are your favorites. You can try it with pears, too. I blend in the peels for added nutrients but, if that's not your thing, peel the apples before cooking.

3 pounds apples, cored
¼ cup freshly squeezed lemon juice

1 teaspoon ground cinnamon

1. In a 4-quart slow cooker, combine the apples, lemon juice, and cinnamon.

2. Cover the slow cooker and cook on low heat for 8 hours.

3. Transfer the mixture to a blender and purée until smooth. Spoon the applesauce into glass jars or an airtight container and refrigerate for up to 5 days or freeze for up to 6 months.

Per Serving (1 cup): Calories: 46; Total Fat: 0g; Sodium: 2mg; Sugars: 9g; Carbohydrates: 12g; Fiber: 2g; Protein: 0g

GLUTEN-FREE
NIGHTSHADE-FREE
NUT-FREE
SOY-FREE
VEGAN

PREP TIME
20 minutes

COOK TIME
8 hours

TOTAL TIME
8 hours, 20 minutes

Variation Tip: Freeze individual portions of applesauce in silicone muffin tins and transfer them to freezer bags for easy use.

ROASTED GARLIC *Serves 12*

Easiest. Spread. Ever! It's a great alternative to butter and it's incredibly delicious. Prepare to be addicted. Spread it on bread or use it as a dip for your favorite crackers or veggies.

3 heads garlic

3 tablespoons olive oil

Bread, such as sourdough, brioche, or Italian, or crackers, for serving

GLUTEN-FREE
NIGHTSHADE-FREE
NUT-FREE
SOY-FREE
VEGAN

PREP TIME
15 minutes
COOK TIME
3 hours
TOTAL TIME
3 hours, 15 minutes

1. Cut off the tops of the garlic heads to expose the cloves.

2. Pour a bit of olive oil into the bottom of a 1-quart slow cooker or into a baking dish inserted into a larger slow cooker. Place the garlic heads, cut-side up, in the slow cooker. Drizzle the remaining olive oil over the garlic.

3. Cover the slow cooker and cook on low heat for 2 to 3 hours, until the garlic is completely soft. It should look golden brown.

4. Using a knife or a spoon, pop the garlic cloves out of their skins and spread them onto your bread.

Per Serving (excluding bread): Calories: 43; Total Fat: 4g; Sodium: 2mg; Sugars: 0g; Carbohydrates: 3g; Fiber: 0g; Protein: 1g

CARAMELIZED ONIONS *Serves 16*

Add these amazing Caramelized Onions to your favorite dip. They are particularly good in hummus or blue cheese spread. Use them in the French Onion Soup (page 71). Yum.

8 onions, or more if needed, halved and thinly sliced

4 tablespoons butter or olive oil

1 teaspoon salt

1. Fill a 6-quart slow cooker with the onions until it's about three-fourths full.

2. Add the butter and salt and toss to combine.

3. Cover the slow cooker and cook on low heat for 10 hours.

4. Stir the onions, re-cover the cooker, and cook on low heat for 5 hours more, stirring occasionally, until the onions are brown and the liquid is nearly gone.

5. The onions can be refrigerated in an airtight container for up to 5 days or frozen for up to 6 months.

Per Serving: Calories: 47; Total Fat: 3g; Sodium: 170mg; Sugars: 2g; Carbohydrates: 5g; Fiber: 1g; Protein: 1g

GLUTEN-FREE
NIGHTSHADE-FREE
NUT-FREE
SOY-FREE

PREP TIME
10 minutes

COOK TIME
15 hours

TOTAL TIME
15 hours, 10 minutes

SAMOSA BITES *Serves 8*

Samosas are a family-favorite treat, but the pastry they are wrapped in can require too much work at times. These bites feature the potato goodness of samosa filling and are still easy enough to make in the slow cooker.

4 baked Yukon gold potatoes, cubed

4 small carrots, peeled and diced

1 green bell pepper, seeded and diced small

1 cup peas

2 tablespoons ground cumin

2 tablespoons chopped fresh cilantro

1 tablespoon ginger paste

1 tablespoon freshly squeezed lemon juice

1 tablespoon garam masala

1 tablespoon ground coriander

1 teaspoon sesame oil

¾ teaspoon salt

½ teaspoon cayenne pepper

½ teaspoon ground turmeric

½ teaspoon garlic powder

½ teaspoon amchur powder (optional)

½ teaspoon chaat masala (optional)

1 tablespoon olive oil

GLUTEN-FREE
NUT-FREE
SOY-FREE
VEGAN

PREP TIME
15 minutes

COOK TIME
6 to 8 hours

TOTAL TIME
8 hours, 15 minutes

Ingredient Tip: Amchur powder is dried mango powder and chaat masala is a spice mixture that also includes amchur powder along with other spices—such as cumin, coriander, asafoetida, and chili powder—and you can find either one in Asian grocery stores or online. If you can't find them, omit them.

1. In a large bowl, combine all of the ingredients except the olive oil. Mash to completely combine. Using your hands, form the mixture into 1½-inch balls.

2. Pour the olive oil into a 4-quart slow cooker. Add the samosa balls.

3. Wrap the lid of the slow cooker in a clean kitchen towel, place it on the slow cooker, and cook on low heat for 6 to 8 hours.

4. If you'd like your samosa bites to be browned and crispy, place the crock under the broiler for a few minutes.

Per Serving: Calories: 141; Total Fat: 3g; Sodium: 253mg; Sugars: 4g; Carbohydrates: 25g; Fiber: 4g; Protein: 4g

WHITE PIZZA DIP   *Serves 8*

This dip is like cheesy tomato-y garlicky crack. I absolutely love it when I get a piece with a lot of roasted garlic. I snuck in some kale and it's officially one of only TWO recipes in existence that I like with that vegetable. I know, I'm vegetarian(ish) and I should love kale, but I just don't. For the curious, the other recipe I like kale in is this Indian Potato-Kale Soup (page 67).

2 cups grape tomatoes, halved

1 pound shredded mozzarella cheese

8 ounces cream cheese, at room temperature

4 ounces shredded kale

¼ cup finely grated Parmesan cheese, plus more for garnish

6 garlic cloves, minced or pressed

1 tablespoon Italian Seasoning (page 33)

1 teaspoon olive oil

¼ teaspoon salt

¼ teaspoon freshly ground black pepper

Crackers, carrots and other veggies, bread, or chips for serving

GLUTEN-FREE
NUT-FREE
SOY-FREE

PREP TIME
10 minutes

COOK TIME
4 hours

TOTAL TIME
4 hours, 10 minutes

1. In a 4-quart slow cooker, stir together the tomatoes, mozzarella cheese, cream cheese, kale, Parmesan cheese, garlic, Italian seasoning, olive oil, salt, and pepper.

2. Cover the slow cooker and cook on low heat for 4 hours.

3. Serve with the crackers, vegetables, or your dippers of choice.

Per Serving: Calories: 319; Total Fat: 26g; Sodium: 498mg; Sugars: 1g; Carbohydrates: 7g; Fiber: 1g; Protein: 16g

HUMMUS *Serves 4 to 6*

My family absolutely loves my homemade Hummus. And once you see how easy it is to make, you'll never buy it at the store again. If you happen to have cooked chickpeas in your refrigerator, you can make this in just a few minutes. Serve this with Falafel (page 96) or the Chickpea Shawarma Rice Bowl (page 119), or use it as an ingredient in Chickpea Nuggets (page 129).

1 cup dried chickpeas

2 garlic cloves, minced

¼ cup avocado oil

2 tablespoons freshly squeezed lime juice

1 tablespoon tahini

1 tablespoon ground cumin

⅛ teaspoon cayenne pepper (optional)

Pita bread or cut-up vegetables, for serving

GLUTEN-FREE
NUT-FREE
SOY-FREE
VEGAN

PREP TIME
10 minutes

COOK TIME
8 hours

TOTAL TIME
8 hours, 10 minutes

1. Cook the chickpeas in the slow cooker following the instructions for Slow-Cooked Beans (page 15). Reserve the cooking liquid.

2. Let the chickpeas cool to room temperature.

3. Transfer the chickpeas to a food processor and add the garlic, avocado oil, lime juice, tahini, cumin, and cayenne (if using). Pulse to combine.

4. With the motor running, add the reserved chickpea cooking liquid, a little at a time, until the hummus reaches your desired consistency.

5. Serve with pita bread or vegetables for dipping.

6. The hummus can be refrigerated in an airtight container for up to 5 days or frozen for up to 6 months.

Per Serving: Calories: 226; Total Fat: 13g; Sodium: 13mg; Sugars: 4g; Carbohydrates: 22g; Fiber: 6g; Protein: 7g

TOMATILLO SALSA *Serves 6*

If you've never had tomatillos, try this recipe. They are the secret to what makes this salsa so delicious. They will be your new favorite fruit. Yes, like tomatoes, they are considered a fruit.

1½ pounds tomatillos, husked

¼ cup minced yellow onion

2 serrano peppers, seeded and roughly chopped

2 garlic cloves, roughly chopped

½ teaspoon kosher salt

¼ teaspoon white pepper

3 tablespoons chopped fresh cilantro

GLUTEN-FREE
NUT-FREE
SOY-FREE
VEGAN

PREP TIME
15 minutes

COOK TIME
8 hours

TOTAL TIME
8 hours, 15 minutes

1. In a 4-quart slow cooker, combine the tomatillos, onion, serranos, garlic, salt, white pepper, and cilantro and stir to combine.

2. Wrap the lid of the slow cooker in a clean kitchen towel, place it on the slow cooker, and cook on low heat for 8 hours.

3. Transfer the mixture to a blender or food processor and purée to your desired consistency. Spoon the salsa into a glass jar or airtight container and chill before serving.

4. The salsa can be refrigerated for up to 5 days or frozen for up to 6 months.

Per Serving: Calories: 41; Total Fat: 1g; Sodium: 196mg; Sugars: 0g; Carbohydrates: 8g; Fiber: 2g; Protein: 1g

SEVEN-LAYER DIP *Serves 8*

Seven-Layer Dip is always a hit at parties and, if you have cooked beans and Yogurt (page 20) already waiting in the fridge, it's easy to make this at the last minute. Serve it with your favorite tortilla chips.

2 cups cooked black beans (see Slow-Cooked Beans, page 15), mashed

2 tablespoons Taco Seasoning (page 32)

2 cups guacamole

1 cup salsa

2 cups shredded Cheddar cheese

2 cups plain Yogurt (page 20), store-bought plain yogurt salted to taste, or sour cream

1 cup sliced black olives

½ cup sliced scallions

2 tablespoons chopped fresh cilantro

Tortilla chips, for serving

GLUTEN-FREE
NUT-FREE
SOY-FREE

PREP TIME
15 minutes

COOK TIME
18 hours

TOTAL TIME
18 hours, 15 minutes

1. Have a 9-by-13-inch baking dish ready.

2. In a medium bowl, stir together the black beans and taco seasoning. Spread them into the baking dish.

3. Spread layers of guacamole and salsa over the beans.

4. Sprinkle on the shredded Cheddar cheese.

5. Spread the yogurt over the cheese and top with the olives, scallions, and cilantro.

6. Serve with a big bowl of tortilla chips.

Per Serving: Calories: 342; Total Fat: 22g; Sodium: 832mg; Sugars: 5g; Carbohydrates: 27g; Fiber: 5g; Protein: 16g

Ingredient Tip: Buy fresh guacamole at your grocery store or make your own with mashed avocado, a splash of freshly squeezed lime juice, diced serrano pepper, and a dash each of ground cumin and salt.

Variation Tip: If you feel like adding an eighth layer, spread on a layer of Mexican rice (see Rice, page 17, Variation Tip).

SOURDOUGH STARTER AND SOURDOUGH BREAD *Serves 8*

Making sourdough bread is definitely a commitment but the result—a light and fluffy loaf full of tangy flavor—is so satisfying. And it bakes up well in the slow cooker. To proof the dough, you'll need a banneton or proofing basket. You can improvise one by lining a colander with a well-floured, clean linen kitchen towel. If you use this, be sure to cut slits into the top of the dough for venting before you bake it. While most of my recipes are measured by volume, here I weigh the solid ingredients using grams, so you'll need a kitchen scale. This gives you more accurate measures and consistent results.

FOR THE SOURDOUGH STARTER

1 kg white bread flour, divided

340 ml (1½ cups) lukewarm water

1 unpeeled apple, cored and grated

FOR THE BREAD

Olive oil, for preparing the bowl

400g flour, plus more for dusting

250g sourdough starter

130 to 175 ml (½ cup plus 2 teaspoons to ¾ cup minus 1 teaspoon) lukewarm water

7.5g salt

NIGHTSHADE-FREE
NUT-FREE
SOY-FREE
VEGAN

PREP TIME
8 days

COOK TIME
1½ to 2 hours

TOTAL TIME
8 days, 2 hours

To make the sourdough starter

1. In a half-gallon or larger airtight container, mix together 500g of flour, the lukewarm water, and grated apple. Mark the level on the outside of the container so you can track how the mixture rises. Cover and let sit at room temperature for 3 days.

2. Discard half the mixture (or use it in pancakes or quick breads by replacing some of the flour and liquid. For example, use ½ cup starter to replace ¼ cup flour and ¼ cup liquid in the batter).

Continued

3. Add 250g of flour and 170 ml of water to the starter and mix together. Cover and let sit at room temperature for 2 more days. You should see bubbles and the mixture should rise significantly above the line you placed on the outside of the container. This means the starter is active.

4. Discard half the mixture again and mix in another 250g of flour and about 170 ml of water to bring it up to the line. Cover and let sit for another 2 days.

5. At this point the starter is ready to use. If you plan to use the starter often, leave it on the counter at room temperature and feed it every 3 days as in step 4. If not, refrigerate it to slow the activity. To revive the starter, bring it to room temperature and feed it 24 hours before you plan to use it.

To make the bread

1. Coat a large bowl and a slow cooker insert with olive oil. Dust a banneton or proofing basket with flour.

2. In the bowl of a stand mixer fitted with the dough hook, mix together the flour and sourdough starter on low speed. Add 130 ml of lukewarm water and mix, adding more water as needed and increasing the speed as needed, for 10 to 15 minutes or until a dough forms. Continue to knead until the dough is smooth and elastic.

3. Transfer the dough to the oiled bowl and cover it with a floured kitchen towel. Let sit at room temperature for 5 hours, or until the dough doubles in size.

4. Add the salt. Knock the air out of the dough and knead it until smooth. Roll the dough into a ball and dust it with flour. Transfer the dough to the floured banneton and let rise at room temperature for 4 to 8 hours. Transfer the dough to the oiled slow cooker.

5. Cover the slow cooker and cook on high heat for 1½ to 2 hours until a firm crust forms and the bread sounds hollow when tapped.

6. To brown the top of the bread, transfer the loaf to the oven and broil for 3 to 5 minutes, watching carefully so it doesn't burn. Let cool for a few minutes before cutting into slices and serving.

Per Serving: Calories: 135; Total Fat: 2g; Sodium: 285mg; Sugars: 0g; Carbohydrates: 27g; Fiber: 1g; Protein: 5g

MASHED CAULIFLOWER   *Serves 5*

Looking for a nutrient-dense side dish that's really tasty, too? This one's a winner. My family absolutely loves it. I bet yours will, too.

1 head cauliflower, stem trimmed and leaves removed

4 tablespoons butter, melted, plus more as needed

2 tablespoons Italian Seasoning (page 33)

4 garlic cloves, minced

1½ teaspoons salt

Grated zest of 1 lemon

Juice of 1 lemon

Heavy (whipping) cream, for mashing (optional)

GLUTEN-FREE
NIGHTSHADE-FREE
NUT-FREE
SOY-FREE

PREP TIME
15 minutes

COOK TIME
5 hours

TOTAL TIME
5 hours, 15 minutes

1. Place the cauliflower in a 4-quart slow cooker.

2. In a small bowl, stir together the melted butter, Italian seasoning, garlic, salt, and lemon zest. Pour the butter mixture over the cauliflower.

3. Pour the lemon juice around the cauliflower.

4. Cover the slow cooker and cook on low heat for 5 hours.

5. Using a potato masher, mash the cauliflower and combine it with the cooking liquid. Add more butter or cream, as desired.

Per Serving: Calories: 133; Total Fat: 11g; Sodium: 802mg; Sugars: 4g; Carbohydrates: 8g; Fiber: 3g; Protein: 3g

ASIAN LETTUCE WRAPS   *Serves 4*

Meaty portobello mushrooms replace meat in these wraps. The sweet and tangy sauce is irresistible.

1 pound portobello mushrooms, diced

1 onion, finely diced

8 ounces water chestnuts, diced

¼ cup coconut aminos or soy sauce

2 tablespoons minced garlic

2 tablespoons rice vinegar

1½ tablespoons molasses

1 tablespoon gochujang or sriracha

1 tablespoon peanut butter

1 tablespoon sesame oil

½ teaspoon freshly ground black pepper

3 scallions, thinly sliced

10 to 12 iceberg or Bibb lettuce leaves

GLUTEN-FREE
SOY-FREE
VEGAN

PREP TIME
10 minutes

COOK TIME
6 to 8 hours

TOTAL TIME
6 to 8 hours, 10 minutes

Ingredient Tip: To make this nightshade-free, leave out the gochujang.

1. In a 4-quart slow cooker, stir together the mushrooms, onion, water chestnuts, coconut aminos, garlic, vinegar, molasses, gochujang, peanut butter, sesame oil, and pepper.

2. Cover the slow cooker and cook on low heat for 6 to 8 hours.

3. Add the scallions and stir to combine.

4. Place 2 large lettuce leaves on a serving plate and spoon the filling over the top.

5. Spoon 2 to 3 tablespoons of filling into individual lettuce leaves and roll up like a burrito.

Per Serving: Calories: 156; Total Fat: 6g; Sodium: 960mg; Sugars: 10g; Carbohydrates: 22g; Fiber: 4g; Protein: 6g

ASIAN BRUSSELS SPROUTS *Serves 6*

How is it that Brussels sprouts got such a bad reputation? I'm convinced it's because people only try them boiled and steamed. The key is roasting or, in this case, slow cooker roasting! Roasting these little gems brings their natural caramelization to the surface and, oh boy, it's a party.

1 pound fresh Brussels sprouts, trimmed and halved

2 garlic cloves, thinly sliced

3 tablespoons sesame oil

3 tablespoons coconut aminos or soy sauce

2 tablespoons maple syrup

2 tablespoons freshly squeezed lemon juice

2 tablespoons white sesame seeds

2 tablespoons black sesame seeds

2 teaspoons gochujang

Kosher salt

GLUTEN-FREE
NUT-FREE
SOY-FREE
VEGAN

PREP TIME
10 minutes

COOK TIME
4 hours

TOTAL TIME
4 hours, 10 minutes

1. In a 2-quart slow cooker, combine the Brussels sprouts, garlic, sesame oil, coconut aminos, maple syrup, lemon juice, white and black sesame seeds, and gochujang. Season with salt.

2. Cover the slow cooker and cook on low heat for 4 hours.

3. Stir well before serving hot.

Per Serving: Calories: 152; Total Fat: 10g; Sodium: 499mg; Sugars: 4g; Carbohydrates: 14g; Fiber: 6g; Protein: 4g

FRESH GREEN BEAN CASSEROLE *Serves 4*

You will love the improved flavors (not to mention the increased nutrients) of using fresh green beans instead of canned for this casserole. Honestly, it's a game changer.

4 tablespoons butter, plus more for preparing the baking dish

1 pound fresh green beans, trimmed and cut into 3-inch pieces

1 cup cooked chickpeas (see Slow-Cooked Beans, page 15; optional)

1⅓ cups French-fried onions, divided

1¾ cups milk

¾ cup Vegetable Scrap Broth (page 14) or store-bought broth

⅓ cup diced onion

½ cup diced mushrooms

¼ cup gluten-free flour

2 garlic cloves, minced

¼ teaspoon salt

GLUTEN-FREE
NIGHTSHADE-FREE
NUT-FREE
SOY-FREE

PREP TIME
15 minutes

COOK TIME
6 to 8 hours

TOTAL TIME
6 hours to 8 hours, 15 minutes

1. Coat a 2-quart slow cooker insert (or a baking dish to fit inside your slow cooker) with butter.

2. Bring a large pot of water to a boil over high heat. Add the green beans and blanch for 30 seconds. Drain and transfer the beans to the prepared slow cooker.

3. Add the chickpeas (if using), ⅔ cup of French-fried onions, the milk, vegetable broth, onion, mushrooms, remaining butter, flour, garlic, and salt. Stir to combine.

4. Cover the slow cooker and cook on low heat for 6 to 8 hours.

5. Sprinkle the remaining ⅔ cup of French-fried onions over the top and, if desired, place the crock under the broiler for a few minutes to crisp them.

Per Serving: Calories: 358; Total Fat: 25g; Sodium: 460mg; Sugars: 8g; Carbohydrates: 30g; Fiber: 4g; Protein: 7g

SPANISH TORTILLA *Serves 8*

Spanish Tortilla, where have you been all my life? I only recently discovered this wonderful egg and potato dish, which is kind of like a frittata or fried rice or a quesadilla, in that you can add leftovers or other random ingredients from the fridge to it and nearly anything will work. Here, I use mushrooms and cilantro, but you could add tomatoes or olives or feta cheese and it will be amazing. It also has the added bonus of looking really fancy, even though it's pretty simple to pull together.

4 tablespoons butter

2 yellow onions, diced

8 ounces portobello mushrooms, diced

1 tablespoon avocado oil

10 large eggs

1 teaspoon salt

1 tablespoon finely chopped fresh cilantro

1 teaspoon finely chopped scallion

3 large baking potatoes, peeled and thinly sliced

¼ teaspoon paprika

GLUTEN-FREE
NUT-FREE
SOY-FREE

PREP TIME
30 minutes

COOK TIME
7 to 8 hours

TOTAL TIME
8 hours, 30 minutes

1. In a skillet over medium-low heat, melt the butter. Add the onions and cook for 15 to 20 minutes, stirring frequently, until caramelized. Add the mushrooms and cook for 5 minutes more.

2. Pour the avocado oil into a 4-quart slow cooker.

3. In a large bowl, whisk the eggs and salt. Stir in the onions and mushrooms, cilantro, and scallion.

4. Place half the potato slices in the bottom of the slow cooker. Top with half the egg mixture. Repeat the layers. Sprinkle the top with paprika.

5. Wrap the lid of the slow cooker in a clean kitchen towel, place it on the slow cooker, and cook on low heat for 7 to 8 hours.

6. Cut into wedges and serve.

Per Serving: Calories: 269; Total Fat: 13g; Sodium: 419mg; Sugars: 4g; Carbohydrates: 28g; Fiber: 3g; Protein: 10g

GERMAN HOT SLAW *Serves 8 to 12*

This is the veganized version of an old family recipe, which originally called for bacon crumbles and animal fat. I've substituted smoked salt for the bacon, and the cabbage and vinegar bring the rest of the deliciousness on their own. If you like your slaw on the sweet side, use the larger quantity of sugar.

2 heads cabbage, thinly sliced

1 cup balsamic vinegar, plus more as needed

2 tablespoons smoked salt, plus more as needed

¼ to ½ cup sugar, plus more as needed

2 tablespoons avocado oil

4 cups water, plus more as needed

GLUTEN-FREE
NIGHTSHADE-FREE
NUT-FREE
SOY-FREE
VEGAN

PREP TIME
15 minutes

COOK TIME
4 hours

TOTAL TIME
4 hours, 15 minutes

1. In a 4-quart slow cooker toss together the cabbage, vinegar, salt, sugar, and avocado oil.

2. Add the water. If your cabbage heads are small, add a little less water; if they are large, add a little more.

3. Cover the slow cooker and cook on low heat for 4 hours, checking on it occasionally. You don't want it to be mushy. It's best when the cabbage still has a little bite.

4. Taste and adjust the salt, sugar, and vinegar levels as needed.

5. The cabbage can be refrigerated in an airtight container for up to 5 days or frozen for up to 6 months.

Per Serving: Calories: 127; Total Fat: 4g; Sodium: 449mg; Sugars: 16g; Carbohydrates: 22g; Fiber: 5g; Protein: 2g

HERBED MASHED POTATOES *Serves 4 to 6*

Creamy, dreamy mashed potatoes . . . what can be better at the holidays? Or, you know, on a Tuesday? These are easy and delicious and you'll want to make them all the time.

4 large red
potatoes, cubed

¾ cup Vegetable Scrap
Broth (page 14) or
store-bought broth

4 ounces cream cheese,
at room temperature

4 tablespoons butter, at
room temperature

1 tablespoon
minced garlic

1 tablespoon Italian
Seasoning (page 33)

Salt

Freshly ground
black pepper

Garlic powder

GLUTEN-FREE
NUT-FREE
SOY-FREE

PREP TIME
10 minutes

COOK TIME
6 to 8 hours

TOTAL TIME
6 to 8 hours, 10 minutes

1. In a 4-quart slow cooker, stir together the red potatoes and vegetable broth.

2. Cover the slow cooker and cook on low heat for 6 to 8 hours until tender.

3. Place a colander over a large bowl and strain the potatoes, reserving the broth. Transfer the potatoes to a large bowl and, using a potato masher, mash them to your desired consistency.

4. In a small bowl, stir together the cream cheese, butter, garlic, and Italian seasoning and season with salt, pepper, and garlic powder. Add the cream cheese mixture to the potatoes and stir to combine, adding some of the reserved vegetable broth if needed to reach your desired consistency. Serve hot.

Per Serving: Calories: 475; Total Fat: 23g; Sodium: 194mg;
Sugars: 5g; Carbohydrates: 61g; Fiber: 6g; Protein: 9g

Taco Soup, page 69

4

SOUPS, STEWS, CHILIS, AND CURRIES

RED LENTIL SOUP   *Serves 8*

Red lentils are the sweetest of all the lentil varieties, compared to brown and green types, and they make a great soup. They also break down after cooking so they are easy to purée, which makes them work well for this recipe. The cumin, lemon, and tomato paste give this soup a slight Mediterranean flavor.

4 cups Vegetable Scrap Broth (page 14) or store-bought broth

2 cups dried red lentils

2 large carrots, peeled and diced

1 onion, chopped

1 tablespoon minced garlic

1 tablespoon tomato paste

1 tablespoon ground cumin

1 teaspoon salt

1 quart water

Juice of ½ lemon

¼ cup chopped fresh cilantro

GLUTEN-FREE
NUT-FREE
SOY-FREE
VEGAN

PREP TIME
10 minutes

COOK TIME
4 to 6 hours

TOTAL TIME
6 hours, 10 minutes

1. In a 4-quart slow cooker, stir together the vegetable broth, lentils, carrots, onion, garlic, tomato paste, cumin, salt, and water until combined.

2. Cover the slow cooker and cook on low heat for 4 to 6 hours.

3. Using an immersion blender, blend the soup in the cooker until smooth. Or transfer the soup to a standard blender, working in batches as needed, and purée.

4. To serve, ladle into bowls, drizzle with lemon juice, and sprinkle with cilantro.

Per Serving: Calories: 198; Total Fat: 1g; Sodium: 328mg; Sugars: 5g; Carbohydrates: 36g; Fiber: 16g; Protein: 13g

BLACK BEAN SOUP *Serves 8*

The best part of this recipe is that you can add just about any combination of vegetables you like—green beans, peas, corn, spinach, or mushrooms (go ahead, use those leftovers in the fridge)—and have a fantastic-tasting soup. In our family, we top our bowls with cheese, avocado, sour cream, and Mexican hot sauce, but feel free to try whatever toppings you like. Soak the black beans the night before and they'll be ready to add to the slow cooker in the morning. By the time you get home for dinner, the soup will be ready.

1 tablespoon olive oil

2 cups dried black beans, soaked in water overnight or up to 10 hours

4 cups Vegetable Scrap Broth (page 14) or store-bought broth

2 cups water

4 large tomatoes, chopped

1 cup chopped vegetables

¼ cup Taco Seasoning (page 32)

Salt

Freshly ground black pepper

Salsa, for serving (optional)

Chopped fresh cilantro, for serving (optional)

GLUTEN-FREE
SOY-FREE
VEGAN

PREP TIME
10 minutes

COOK TIME
8 to 10 hours on low / 4 to 6 hours on high

TOTAL TIME
4 to 10 hours, 10 minutes

Variation Tip: Make this in your pressure cooker by cooking it for 30 minutes on the Bean setting and letting the pressure release naturally.

1. Pour the olive oil into a 6-quart slow cooker.

2. Drain the black beans and add them to the slow cooker, along with the vegetable broth, water, tomatoes, vegetables, and taco seasoning. Season with salt and pepper and stir to combine.

3. Cover the slow cooker and cook on low heat for 8 to 10 hours.

4. Using an immersion blender, blend the soup until smooth. Or transfer the soup to a standard blender, working in batches as needed, and purée.

5. Ladle the soup into bowls and top with salsa and chopped cilantro (if using).

Per Serving: Calories: 239; Total Fat: 3g; Sodium: 321mg; Sugars: 7g; Carbohydrates: 43g; Fiber: 9g; Protein: 12g

MINESTRONE *Serves 8*

Minestrone takes a little more work to prepare with fresh ingredients rather than canned, but the superior flavors of roasted corn and fresh tomatoes are worth the effort.

1 tablespoon olive oil

4 cups Vegetable Scrap Broth (page 14) or store-bought broth

2 cups cooked black beans (see Slow-Cooked Beans, page 15)

2 cups diced Roma tomato

1 cup fresh corn, roasted

8 ounces mushrooms, sliced

2 teaspoons salt

1 teaspoon minced garlic

2 cups water

GLUTEN-FREE
NUT-FREE
SOY-FREE
VEGAN

PREP TIME
10 minutes

COOK TIME
6 to 8 hours

TOTAL TIME
6 to 8 hours, 10 minutes

1. In a 6-quart slow cooker, stir together the olive oil, vegetable broth, black beans, tomato, corn, mushrooms, salt, garlic, and water.

2. Cover the slow cooker and cook on low heat for 6 to 8 hours.

Per Serving: Calories: 114; Total Fat: 3g; Sodium: 746mg; Sugars: 4g; Carbohydrates: 18g; Fiber: 5g; Protein: 6g

CREAMY PORTOBELLO SOUP *Serves 4*

This is not cream of mushroom soup. While that soup is a lovely tool for casseroles and the like, it's not a very exciting meal to be eaten alone. But this Creamy Portobello Soup features the mighty mushroom in all its umami glory. You can serve this soup as a main course or as a side for Trinity Beet Burgers with Goat Cheese and Arugula (page 98).

6 cups (about 1 pound) chopped portobello mushrooms

1½ cups coconut milk

¼ cup coconut oil

1 teaspoon chopped garlic

1 teaspoon salt

Freshly ground black pepper

Cayenne pepper

1 cup chopped scallions

GLUTEN-FREE
NUT-FREE
SOY-FREE
VEGAN

PREP TIME
15 minutes

COOK TIME
8 hours

TOTAL TIME
8 hours, 15 minutes

1. In a 4-quart slow cooker, stir together the mushrooms, coconut milk, coconut oil, garlic, and salt and season with black pepper and cayenne.

2. Cover the slow cooker and cook on low heat for 8 hours.

3. Add half the scallions.

4. Using an immersion blender, purée the soup in the cooker. Or transfer to a standard blender, working in batches as needed, and blend until smooth.

5. Ladle the soup into bowls and top with the remaining scallions.

Per Serving: Calories: 360; Total Fat: 35g; Sodium: 599mg; Sugars: 4g; Carbohydrates: 11g; Fiber: 4g; Protein: 7g

TOMATO SOUP WITH PASTA STARS *Serves 4*

Tomato soup is a comfort food staple and we love to make ours with veggies, a bit of cream, and pasta stars. Use this recipe as a jumping-off point to create your favorite way to serve tomato soup. Serve it with grilled cheese sandwiches made with homemade Sourdough Bread (page 49) for the ultimate cold-day comfort meal.

2 tomatoes, diced, or 1 (14.5-ounce can) diced tomatoes

2 cups frozen vegetable blend

1 cup Vegetable Scrap Broth (page 14) or store-bought broth

¾ cup olive oil

1 small carrot, peeled and diced

¼ cup chopped fresh basil leaves

1 yellow onion, diced

2 garlic cloves, minced

1 bay leaf

Salt

Freshly ground black pepper

½ cup dried star or alphabet pasta

½ cup heavy (whipping) cream

2 tablespoons butter

SOY-FREE
NUT-FREE

PREP TIME
10 minutes

COOK TIME
6 hours

TOTAL TIME
6 hours, 10 minutes

1. In a 4-quart slow cooker, stir together the tomatoes, frozen vegetables, vegetable broth, olive oil, carrot, basil, onion, garlic, and bay leaf and season with salt and pepper.

2. Cover the slow cooker and cook on low heat for 6 hours.

3. Stir in the pasta, heavy cream, and butter. Re-cover the cooker and cook on high heat for 15 minutes more. Serve hot.

Per Serving: Calories: 579; Total Fat: 55g; Sodium: 85mg; Sugars: 7g; Carbohydrates: 22g; Fiber: 3g; Protein: 4g

BUTTERNUT-POBLANO SOUP *Serves 8*

Butternut squash, the fantastic winter cousin of the pumpkin, pairs happily with the slightly spicy, flavorful poblano pepper in this creamy, rich winter soup. Because butternut squash is a good source of fiber, vitamin C, magnesium, and potassium, it's not only delicious but also a nutritious choice for your soup base.

1 butternut squash, peeled and cubed

1 poblano pepper, roughly chopped

1¼ cups diced onion

2 cups Vegetable Scrap Broth (page 14) or store-bought broth

6 tablespoons minced garlic

2 tablespoons gluten-free flour

½ tablespoon salt

1 tablespoon chili powder

1 tablespoon dried parsley

1 teaspoon freshly ground black pepper

1 teaspoon ground coriander

¼ teaspoon ground cinnamon

⅛ teaspoon dried rosemary

3 cups milk

8 tablespoons (1 stick) butter

GLUTEN-FREE
NUT-FREE
SOY-FREE

PREP TIME
15 minutes

COOK TIME
8 hours, 30 minutes

TOTAL TIME
8 hours, 45 minutes

1. In a 6-quart slow cooker, stir together the squash, poblano, onion, vegetable broth, garlic, flour, salt, chili powder, parsley, pepper, coriander, cinnamon, and rosemary.

2. Cover the slow cooker and cook on low heat for 8 hours.

3. Using an immersion blender, blend the soup in the cooker until smooth. Or transfer the soup to a standard blender, working in batches as needed, and purée. Pour the soup back into the slow cooker, if using the standard blender.

4. Add the milk and butter. Re-cover the cooker and cook for 30 minutes more.

Per Serving: Calories: 225; Total Fat: 14g; Sodium: 584mg; Sugars: 9g; Carbohydrates: 24g; Fiber: 3g; Protein: 5g

CURRY-ROASTED CAULIFLOWER SOUP *Serves 8*

This recipe started out as a roasted-in-the-oven adventure and evolved once I realized I could "roast" the cauliflower in the slow cooker. If you find it doesn't get quite roasted enough for you, simply pop it under your broiler for a few minutes before adding the broth in step 6.

2 tablespoons coconut oil, melted

1 tablespoon curry powder, plus more as needed

1 teaspoon salt

1 head cauliflower, cut into florets

1 onion, cut into thin rings

3 cups Vegetable Scrap Broth (page 14) or store-bought broth, divided

GLUTEN-FREE
NUT-FREE
SOY-FREE
VEGAN

PREP TIME
15 minutes

COOK TIME
6 to 8 hours, 15 minutes

TOTAL TIME
6 to 8 hours, 30 minutes

Per Serving: Calories: 61; Total Fat: 4g; Sodium: 325mg; Sugars: 4g; Carbohydrates: 7g; Fiber: 2g; Protein: 2g

1. In a large bowl, stir together the coconut oil, curry powder, and salt.

2. Add the cauliflower and toss with the coconut oil mixture to coat.

3. Place the onion rings in the bottom of a 4-quart slow cooker.

4. Add the cauliflower florets to the slow cooker and pour in ½ cup of the vegetable broth.

5. Wrap the lid of the slow cooker in a clean kitchen towel, place it on the slow cooker, and cook on low heat for 6 to 8 hours, until the onions are caramelized and the cauliflower is roasted.

6. Add the remaining 2½ cups of broth. Re-cover the cooker and cook on high heat for 15 minutes more.

7. If you like a smoother texture, blend some of the cauliflower and onions using an immersion blender or standard blender and stir them back into the soup.

8. Ladle into bowls and serve.

INDIAN POTATO-KALE SOUP *Serves 8*

Tender red potatoes and kale together in a creamy, subtly spiced soup fortified with the umami of miso. Umami is one of the five basic flavors: sweet, salty, sour, bitter, and umami. It is the flavor we think of as savory, or meaty, and there is lots of it in miso and other soy products. If you are dairy-free or vegan, use dairy-free milk.

1 tablespoon olive oil

6 cups chopped kale

4 cups diced red potato

4 cups Vegetable Scrap Broth (page 14) or store-bought broth

1¼ cups diced onion

1 tablespoon miso paste

1 teaspoon minced garlic

½ teaspoon dried thyme

¼ teaspoon dry mustard

⅛ teaspoon salt

⅛ teaspoon freshly ground black pepper

2 cups milk

NUT-FREE

PREP TIME
15 minutes

COOK TIME
5 to 6 hours, 15 minutes

TOTAL TIME
6 hours, 30 minutes

1. In a 6-quart slow cooker, stir together the olive oil, kale, red potato, vegetable broth, onion, miso paste, garlic, thyme, mustard, salt, and pepper.

2. Cover the slow cooker and cook on low heat for 5 to 6 hours.

3. Stir in the milk. Re-cover the cooker and cook on high heat for 15 minutes more. Serve hot.

Per Serving: Calories: 144; Total Fat: 3g; Sodium: 184mg; Sugars: 7g; Carbohydrates: 25g; Fiber: 3g; Protein: 6g

POTATO SOUP *Serves 4*

Potatoes get a bit of a bad rap, nutritionally, but they are filled with phytonutrients, including carotenoids, flavonoids, and caffeic acid, which are believed to promote overall health. The vitamin C in potatoes is an antioxidant, which can help prevent cell damage, and potatoes may also help lower blood pressure. Now, does this mean you should chow down daily on baskets of fries? No. But eating a bowl of potato soup or a baked potato as part of a balanced diet? Go for it.

5 cups Vegetable Scrap Broth (page 14) or store-bought broth

4 potatoes, diced

2 cups diced onion

1 bell pepper, any color, seeded and diced

2 garlic cloves, minced

1 cup milk

½ cup diced mushrooms

4 tablespoons butter

¼ cup gluten-free flour

8 ounces cream cheese

Shredded Cheddar cheese, for serving

Sliced scallions, for serving

GLUTEN-FREE
NUT-FREE
SOY-FREE

PREP TIME
15 minutes

COOK TIME
5 to 6 hours, 30 minutes

TOTAL TIME
6 hours, 45 minutes

1. In a 4-quart slow cooker, stir together the vegetable broth, potatoes, onion, bell pepper, garlic, milk, mushrooms, butter, and flour.

2. Cover the slow cooker and cook on low heat for 5 to 6 hours.

3. Add the cream cheese. Re-cover the cooker and cook on high heat for 30 minutes more.

4. Ladle the soup into bowls and top with the shredded Cheddar cheese and sliced scallions.

Per Serving: Calories: 563; Total Fat: 33g; Sodium: 338mg; Sugars: 16g; Carbohydrates: 58g; Fiber: 7g; Protein: 13g

TACO SOUP *Serves 4*

Our family loves tacos. In fact, we plan our meals in such a way that we have theme nights (Salad Wednesdays, Chickpea Thursdays, Leftovers Weekends). Tuesdays are for tacos. And even though it's not a proper taco, we often have Taco Soup. Just picture all the ingredients you would normally put into a taco shell, add broth, and you pretty much have this delicious soup.

4 cups Vegetable Scrap Broth (page 14) or store-bought broth

1 (14.5-ounce) can corn, undrained

1 (14.5-ounce) can diced tomatoes, with juice, or 2 cups diced fresh tomato

1 cup dried lentils

1 cup dried black beans

1 (7-ounce) can green chilies

2 tablespoons Taco Seasoning (page 32)

Shredded Cheddar cheese, for serving (optional)

Yogurt (page 20), store-bought plain yogurt, or sour cream, for serving (optional)

Chopped fresh cilantro, for serving (optional)

GLUTEN-FREE
NUT-FREE
SOY-FREE

PREP TIME
15 minutes

COOK TIME
8 hours

TOTAL TIME
8 hours, 15 minutes

1. In a 4-quart slow cooker, stir together the vegetable broth, corn, tomatoes, lentils, black beans, green chilies, and taco seasoning.

2. Cover the slow cooker and cook on low heat for 8 hours.

3. Ladle the soup into bowls and top with shredded Cheddar cheese, yogurt, and cilantro (if using).

Per Serving: Calories: 453; Total Fat: 2g; Sodium: 318mg; Sugars: 13g; Carbohydrates: 86g; Fiber: 25g; Protein: 26g

LASAGNA SOUP *Serves 8*

Lasagna can be a lot of work but you can get all those wonderful flavors in a soup that is the easiest thing in the world to make. No need to layer anything. Just toss the ingredients into the slow cooker, leave it to cook all day, and when you get home, be greeted by soup that reminds you of lasagna and joy.

2 quarts Vegetable Scrap Broth (page 14) or store-bought broth

1 (28-ounce) can diced tomatoes

1½ cups dried brown lentils

2 onions, finely chopped

4 garlic cloves, minced

2 cups shredded mozzarella cheese

8 ounces ricotta

½ cup grated Parmesan cheese

½ cup finely chopped fresh basil

2 tablespoons tomato paste

2 teaspoons olive oil

2 teaspoons dried oregano

½ teaspoon red pepper flakes

¼ teaspoon salt

2 bay leaves

Pinch freshly ground black pepper

8 ounces brown rice rotini pasta

GLUTEN-FREE
SOY-FREE
NUT-FREE

PREP TIME
15 minutes

COOK TIME
8 hours, 15 minutes

TOTAL TIME
8 hours, 30 minutes

1. In a 6-quart slow cooker, stir together the vegetable broth, tomatoes, lentils, onions, garlic, mozzarella cheese, ricotta, Parmesan cheese, basil, tomato paste, olive oil, oregano, red pepper flakes, salt, bay leaves, and pepper.

2. Cover the slow cooker and cook on low heat for 8 hours.

3. Add the pasta. Re-cover the cooker, turn the heat to high, and cook for 15 minutes more, or until the pasta is done.

Per Serving: Calories: 413; Total Fat: 11g; Sodium: 583mg; Sugars: 7g; Carbohydrates: 56g; Fiber: 15g; Protein: 25g

FRENCH ONION SOUP *Serves 8*

There are days when only the caramelized onions, bubbly Gruyère, and toasty goodness of French Onion Soup will satisfy. This version of the classic soup uses vegetable broth, which turns this into a hearty and nutritious main dish.

2 tablespoons olive oil, plus more for brushing

6 yellow onions (about 3¼ pounds), halved and cut into slices

10 slices Sourdough Bread (page 49) or other hearty bread, cut into ½-inch-thick slices

½ teaspoon salt, plus more for seasoning

2 cups Vegetable Scrap Broth (page 14) or store-bought broth

½ teaspoon dried thyme

¼ cup dry sherry

6 ounces shredded Gruyère cheese

NIGHTSHADE-FREE
NUT-FREE
SOY-FREE

PREP TIME
25 minutes

COOK TIME
6 hours

TOTAL TIME
6 hours, 25 minutes

Ingredient Tip: If you already have Caramelized Onions (page 42) on hand, skip to step 3 and you'll save a lot of time.

Per Serving: Calories: 367; Total Fat: 12g; Sodium: 603mg; Sugars: 11g; Carbohydrates: 51g; Fiber: 5g; Protein: 15g

1. In a 6-quart slow cooker, stir together the olive oil and onions.

2. Cover the slow cooker and cook on high heat for 5 hours, until the onions are golden.

3. Preheat the oven or a toaster oven to 400°F.

4. Brush the bread slices with olive oil, sprinkle with salt, and toast until golden, about 15 minutes.

5. In a saucepan over medium-low heat, cook the vegetable broth until hot.

6. Stir in the thyme, sherry, and ½ teaspoon of salt. Pour the mixture into the slow cooker with the onions.

7. Arrange the toasted bread slices over the onions and broth in the slow cooker.

8. Sprinkle the Gruyère cheese over the bread.

9. Cover the slow cooker and cook on high heat for about 15 minutes until the cheese is melted. If you like, place the crock under the broiler for a few minutes to get the cheese nice and brown.

10. Ladle into bowls and serve.

TOM KHA GAI *Serves 6*

Most Thai restaurants serve a chicken version of this delicious coconut and lemongrass soup. I have found some places that serve a vegetarian version, but it's relatively rare, so I created this recipe. I think it's pretty great.

2 stalks lemongrass, tough outer leaves removed

3 cups Vegetable Scrap Broth (page 14) or store-bought broth

2 cups cooked chickpeas (see Slow-Cooked Beans, page 15; optional)

1 (13.5-ounce) can coconut milk

½ cup chopped fresh cilantro, plus more for garnish

¼ cup miso paste

4 ounces shiitake mushrooms, cut into slices

3 large carrots, peeled and thinly sliced

3 Thai chiles, thinly sliced

1 shallot, thinly sliced

1 (2-inch) piece fresh galangal or fresh ginger, peeled and grated

6 kaffir lime leaves

2 tablespoons chopped fresh Thai basil

1 scallion, sliced

Grated zest of ½ lime

Juice of ½ lime

Chili oil, for serving

NUT-FREE
VEGAN

PREP TIME
15 minutes
COOK TIME
6 to 8 hours
TOTAL TIME
6 to 8 hours, 15 minutes

Ingredient Tip: Galangal is similar to ginger, but it has a stronger, sharper flavor. If you can't find it, ginger is a fine substitute. Dried kaffir lime leaves can be purchased online if you can't find them at your grocery store. Thai chiles are quite hot, so use them sparingly unless you love spicy soup. Thai basil has purple stems and smells more like anise than regular basil.

1. Using a mallet or a heavy skillet, smash the lemongrass and place it into a 4-quart slow cooker.

2. Add the vegetable broth, chickpeas (if using), coconut milk, cilantro, miso paste, mushrooms, carrots, chiles, shallot, galangal, lime leaves, Thai basil, scallion, lime zest, and lime juice. Stir to combine.

3. Cover the slow cooker and cook on low heat for 6 to 8 hours.

4. Ladle the soup into bowls, top with additional cilantro, and serve with chili oil.

Per Serving: Calories: 204; Total Fat: 16g; Sodium: 664mg; Sugars: 8g; Carbohydrates: 15g; Fiber: 4g; Protein: 4g

PHỞ   *Serves 6 to 8*

Phở, pronounced "fuh," is a Vietnamese soup that is all the rage and, though you can find it in many flavors in the big city, it's hard to find a vegan option where I live out in the 'burbs. So now I make my own portobello version at home.

1 tablespoon whole coriander seeds

1 teaspoon whole cloves

2 whole star anise

2 cardamom pods

1 teaspoon fennel seeds

1 pound portobello mushrooms, cut into slices

1 onion, quartered

1 (4-inch) piece fresh ginger, peeled and grated

1 (2-inch) piece fresh galangal, peeled and grated

2 tablespoons miso paste

6 cups water

1 pound flat rice noodles

Chopped fresh Thai basil, for serving

Chopped fresh cilantro, for serving

Chopped fresh chives, for serving

Lime wedges, for serving (optional)

Thinly sliced Thai chiles, for serving (optional)

Sriracha, for serving (optional)

NUT-FREE
VEGAN

PREP TIME
10 minutes

COOK TIME
8 hours

TOTAL TIME
8 hours, 10 minutes

Ingredient Tip: If you can't find galangal, use fresh ginger in the same amount.

1. In a small skillet over medium-high heat, combine the coriander seeds, cloves, star anise, cardamom pods, and fennel seeds. Toast for about 3 minutes until fragrant. Transfer the spices to a 6-quart slow cooker.

2. Add the mushrooms, onion, ginger, galangal, miso paste, and water and stir to combine.

3. Cover the slow cooker and cook on low heat for 8 hours.

4. Place a colander over a large bowl and strain the broth. Remove and set aside the mushroom and onion pieces. Discard the spices.

Continued

5. In a large saucepan, cook the rice noodles according to the package instructions. Drain and divide the noodles into individual bowls.

6. Spoon the mushrooms and onion over the noodles and ladle the broth over the top. Garnish with your choice of chopped basil, cilantro, or chives. Serve with the limes, fresh chiles, or sriracha on the side (if using).

Per Serving: Calories: 315; Total Fat: 1g; Sodium: 352mg; Sugars: 1g; Carbohydrates: 70g; Fiber: 3g; Protein: 6g

VEGETABLE CHOWDER *Serves 8*

Our little family has been making this delicious Vegetable Chowder since our early days and we usually serve it with blue cheese biscuits (simple—mix chunks of blue cheese into your favorite biscuit recipe). The soup is creamy, herby, chock-full of healthy vegetables, and can be made vegan if you swap in dairy-free ingredients. It's a winner on any night, but it's especially fantastic on cool fall or winter nights.

3 cups Vegetable Scrap Broth (page 14) or store-bought broth

1 cup chopped cauliflower

1 cup diced peeled carrot

1 cup chopped broccoli

½ cup chopped red bell pepper

½ cup chopped onion

½ cup almond flour

4 tablespoons butter or ghee

1 tablespoon chopped fresh parsley

Salt

Freshly ground black pepper

3 cups shredded Cheddar cheese

1½ cups milk

GLUTEN-FREE
SOY-FREE

PREP TIME
15 minutes

COOK TIME
8 hours, 15 minutes

TOTAL TIME
8 hours, 30 minutes

1. In a 6-quart slow cooker, stir together the vegetable broth, cauliflower, carrot, broccoli, red bell pepper, onion, almond flour, butter, and parsley and season with salt and pepper.

2. Cover the slow cooker and cook on low heat for 8 hours.

3. Stir in the Cheddar cheese and milk. Re-cover the cooker and cook on high heat for 15 minutes more.

4. Ladle into bowls and serve.

Per Serving: Calories: 290; Total Fat: 23g; Sodium: 358mg; Sugars: 6g; Carbohydrates: 10g; Fiber: 2g; Protein: 14g

CORN CHOWDER *Serves 4*

There's a reason everyone slathers butter on their corn and this recipe for creamy Corn Chowder proves, once again, that dairy and corn are a perfect pair. If you really want to amp up the rich and creamy style, swap out half the milk for heavy (whipping) cream.

1 tablespoon olive oil

4 cups Vegetable Scrap Broth (page 14) or store-bought broth

4 carrots, peeled and diced

2 large potatoes, diced

2 cups fresh corn kernels

1 onion, diced

1 bell pepper, any color, diced

2 cups milk

Salt

Freshly ground black pepper

GLUTEN-FREE
NUT-FREE
SOY-FREE

PREP TIME
15 minutes

COOK TIME
8 hours, 30 minutes

TOTAL TIME
8 hours, 45 minutes

Variation Tip: To make the soup vegan, use dairy-free milk (such as Dairy-Free Milk, page 21).

1. In a 4-quart slow cooker, combine the olive oil, vegetable broth, carrots, potatoes, corn, onion, and bell pepper.

2. Cover the slow cooker and cook on low heat for 8 hours.

3. Using an immersion blender, blend the soup in the cooker until smooth. Or transfer the mixture to a standard blender, working in batches as needed, and purée. Pour the mixture back into the slow cooker.

4. Add the milk. Re-cover the cooker and cook on high heat for 30 minutes more.

5. Stir, taste, and season with salt and pepper.

Per Serving: Calories: 346; Total Fat: 7g; Sodium: 158mg; Sugars: 21g; Carbohydrates: 65g; Fiber: 9g; Protein: 11g

SICILIAN PORTOBELLO STEW *Serves 8*

This simmering masterpiece is reminiscent of your grandmother's pasta sauce combined with fennel and mushrooms, creating a rich, herby stew that's perfect for the slow cooker's flavor-enriching prowess. The orange zest brightens the stew from what would otherwise be a heavy, rich dish to an amazing, enlightening treat for the palate.

2 pounds portobello mushrooms, cut into slices

1 (28-ounce) can diced tomatoes, with juice

1 fennel bulb, cut into ½-inch wedges

6 shallots, thinly sliced

1 cup green olives, cut into slices

½ cup red wine

1 teaspoon dried rosemary

Grated zest of 1 orange

Salt

Freshly ground black pepper

Herbed Mashed Potatoes (page 57), for serving (optional)

GLUTEN-FREE
NUT-FREE
SOY-FREE
VEGAN

PREP TIME
5 minutes

COOK TIME
4 to 6 hours

TOTAL TIME
6 hours, 5 minutes

1. In a 6-quart slow cooker, stir together the mushrooms, tomatoes and juice, fennel, shallots, olives, red wine, rosemary, and orange zest and season with salt and pepper.

2. Cover the slow cooker and cook on low heat for 4 to 6 hours.

3. Spoon over the mashed potatoes (if using).

Per Serving: Calories: 88; Total Fat: 2g; Sodium: 172mg; Sugars: 5g; Carbohydrates: 14g; Fiber: 4g; Protein: 4g

IRISH STOUT AND 'SHROOM STEW

Serves 8

My family visited Ireland and fell in love with Irish stout and beef stew. This vegetarian version with portobello mushrooms makes great use of the slow cooker and is a stick-to-your-ribs masterpiece I absolutely adore.

2 tablespoons olive oil

2 tablespoons gluten-free flour

1¾ cups Vegetable Scrap Broth (page 14) or store-bought broth, divided

6 Yukon gold potatoes, cut into ½-inch cubes

6 carrots, peeled and chopped

1 pound portobello mushrooms, diced

½ cup Irish stout or real sugar cola

1 onion, diced

¼ cup chopped prunes

2 tablespoons tomato paste

1 teaspoon ground sage

Juice of 1 lemon

Salt

Freshly ground black pepper

¼ cup chopped fresh parsley

Herbed Mashed Potatoes (page 57), for serving (optional)

NUT-FREE
SOY-FREE
VEGAN

PREP TIME
15 minutes

COOK TIME
6 to 8 hours

TOTAL TIME
6 to 8 hours, 15 minutes

1. Pour the olive oil into a 6-quart slow cooker.

2. In a small bowl, stir together the flour and about ½ cup of vegetable broth to make a slurry and add it to the slow cooker.

3. Add the remaining 1¼ cups broth, the potatoes, carrots, mushrooms, stout, onion, prunes, tomato paste, sage, and lemon juice and season with salt and pepper.

4. Cover the slow cooker and cook on low heat for 6 to 8 hours.

5. Ladle the stew into bowls and garnish with chopped parsley. Serve with mashed potatoes (if using).

Per Serving: Calories: 209; Total Fat: 4g; Sodium: 58mg; Sugars: 9g; Carbohydrates: 40g; Fiber: 7g; Protein: 5g

CHICKPEA DORO WAT STEW *Serves 4*

Doro wat is an Ethiopian curry dish, usually made with chicken or lamb and a variety of vegetables. The true key to this dish is the spice blend, called berbere, which usually includes chile peppers, garlic, ginger, and fenugreek.

1 cup dried chickpeas

1 (28-ounce) can diced tomatoes

1 cup water

2 cups Vegetable Scrap Broth (page 14) or store-bought broth

3 onions, halved and cut into slices

6 garlic cloves, minced

1 (2-inch) piece fresh ginger, peeled and grated

¼ cup Berbere Seasoning (page 34)

2 tablespoons ghee

1 cinnamon stick

3 cardamom pods, crushed

Salt

Freshly ground black pepper

GLUTEN-FREE
NUT-FREE
SOY-FREE

PREP TIME
5 minutes

COOK TIME
4 hours

TOTAL TIME
4 hours, 5 minutes

1. In a 4-quart slow cooker, stir together the chickpeas, tomatoes, water, vegetable broth, onions, garlic, ginger, berbere seasoning, ghee, cinnamon stick, and cardamom pods and season with salt and pepper.

2. Cover the slow cooker and cook on low heat for 4 hours.

3. Remove and discard the cinnamon stick. Ladle the soup into bowls and serve.

Per Serving: Calories: 326; Total Fat: 10g; Sodium: 96mg; Sugars: 17g; Carbohydrates: 50g; Fiber: 13g; Protein: 13g

INDIAN BUTTER CHICKPEAS *Serves 4*

You'll find butter chicken at nearly every Indian restaurant you visit but, to make it vegetarian, I've created this recipe for Butter Chickpeas. This curry is milder than most, which means kids really like it, too.

2 cups Vegetable Scrap Broth (page 14) or store-bought broth

½ cup dried chickpeas

2 cups tomato purée

5 Hatch chiles, chopped

6 whole black peppercorns

4 whole cloves

3 cardamom pods

1 cinnamon stick

2 tablespoons olive oil

2 tablespoons honey

3 tablespoons minced garlic

3 tablespoons ginger paste

1 tablespoon plus 1 teaspoon chili powder

1 tablespoon freshly squeezed lemon juice

1 teaspoon paprika

1 teaspoon ground garam masala

1 teaspoon salt

1 cup Yogurt (page 20) or store-bought plain yogurt

1 cup heavy (whipping) cream

4 tablespoons butter

Cayenne pepper

Chopped fresh cilantro, for garnish

Cooked Rice (page 17) or cauliflower rice, for serving (optional)

GLUTEN-FREE
NUT-FREE
SOY-FREE

PREP TIME
15 minutes

COOK TIME
8 hours

TOTAL TIME
8 hours, 15 minutes

Ingredient Tip: Hatch chiles are a type of mild New Mexico chile with a lightly sweet, smoky flavor.

1. In a 4-quart slow cooker, stir together the vegetable broth and chickpeas.

2. In a food processor, combine the tomato purée, chiles, black peppercorns, cloves, cardamom pods, cinnamon stick, olive oil, honey, garlic, ginger paste, chili powder, lemon juice, paprika, garam masala, and salt. Process into a sauce and stir it into the chickpea mixture.

3. Cover the slow cooker and cook on low heat for 8 hours.

Continued

4. Add the yogurt, heavy cream, and butter and stir to combine. Re-cover the slow cooker and cook for 15 minutes more. Taste and season with cayenne and garnish with fresh cilantro.

5. Serve over rice or cauliflower rice (if using).

Per Serving: Calories: 580; Total Fat: 44g; Sodium: 799mg; Sugars: 18g; Carbohydrates: 38g; Fiber: 7g; Protein: 11g

INDIAN OKRA AND TOMATO SAUCE (BHINDI MASALA) *Serves 4*

Also known as *bhindi masala*, this stew combines okra and tomatoes, a classic combination in American cuisine of the South as well. Combined with warm Indian spices, this dish is a unique treat. If using fresh okra, be sure to wash it properly, as it can be slimy if you don't fully wash off the natural mucilage on the surface.

1 tablespoon olive oil

1 pound fresh or frozen okra, washed and cut into slices

1 cup diced tomato

2 tablespoons ground coriander

3 teaspoons minced garlic

2 teaspoons chili powder

1 teaspoon ground cumin

1 teaspoon garam masala

½ teaspoon salt

½ teaspoon ground turmeric

2 cups cooked Rice (page 17), for serving

GLUTEN-FREE
NUT-FREE
SOY-FREE
VEGAN

PREP TIME
10 minutes

COOK TIME
4 to 6 hours

TOTAL TIME
6 hours, 10 minutes

1. In a 4-quart slow cooker, stir together the olive oil, okra, tomato, coriander, garlic, chili powder, cumin, garam masala, salt, and turmeric.

2. Cover the slow cooker and cook on low heat for 4 to 6 hours.

3. Serve over rice.

Per Serving: Calories: 215; Total Fat: 4g; Sodium: 317mg; Sugars: 3g; Carbohydrates: 39g; Fiber: 5g; Protein: 5g

CHICKPEA AND VEGETABLE JAMBALAYA *Serves 8*

Jambalaya is a stew originating from Louisiana and it is usually filled with meat and seafood. I dreamed up this veggie-packed version with chickpeas, portobellos, and miso paste in lieu of chicken, sausage, and shrimp.

1 tablespoon olive oil

1 (28-ounce) can diced tomatoes, with juice

8 ounces portobello mushrooms, diced

1 cup Vegetable Scrap Broth (page 14) or store-bought broth

1 cup cooked chickpeas

2 large carrots, peeled and diced

½ large onion, chopped

½ large green bell pepper, seeded and chopped

2 garlic cloves, minced

1 tablespoon miso paste

1½ teaspoons Cajun or Creole spice mix

½ teaspoon dried thyme

½ teaspoon dried oregano

1 cup raw rice

Chopped fresh parsley, for serving (optional)

NUT-FREE
VEGAN

PREP TIME
15 minutes

COOK TIME
4 hours, 20 minutes

TOTAL TIME
4 hours, 35 minutes

Ingredient Tip: Cajun and Creole spice mixes usually contain paprika, garlic powder, onion powder, oregano, cayenne pepper, thyme, basil, salt, and black pepper and can be found in most grocery stores. Depending on the amount of cayenne pepper they contain, these mixes can pack a spicy punch.

1. In a 4-quart slow cooker, stir together the olive oil, tomatoes with juice, mushrooms, vegetable broth, chickpeas, carrots, onion, green bell pepper, garlic, miso paste, Cajun spice mix, thyme, and oregano.

2. Cover the slow cooker and cook on low heat for 4 hours.

3. Add the rice. Re-cover the cooker and cook on high heat for 15 to 20 minutes, or until the rice is done.

4. Spoon into bowls and sprinkle with parsley (if using).

Per Serving: Calories: 237; Total Fat: 4g; Sodium: 152mg; Sugars: 8g; Carbohydrates: 43g; Fiber: 7g; Protein: 9g

BLACK BEAN–LENTIL CHILI *Serves 8*

Vegan chili is a mainstay at our house. We all personalize our bowls with whatever toppings we like, including avocado, hot sauce, and tortilla chips.

I highly recommend making this a day ahead, as the beans are extra delicious after stewing in the spice blend overnight. The leftovers can also be turned into new dishes like chili-cheese mac (see Real Food Mac and Cheese Sauce, page 25), chili quesadillas, chili-topped black bean burgers, chili-topped loaded baked potatoes (see Build Your Own Loaded Baked Potatoes page 112), and chili nachos.

Nonstick cooking spray

4 cups cooked black beans (see Slow-Cooked Beans, page 15)

4 large tomatoes, diced

1 onion, chopped

1 green bell pepper, seeded and chopped

2 cups dried lentils

1 cup Vegetable Scrap Broth (page 14), store-bought broth, or water

3 tablespoons chili powder

2 teaspoons ground cumin

1 teaspoon minced garlic

1 teaspoon freshly ground black pepper

1 teaspoon salt

¼ teaspoon cayenne pepper

Sliced avocado, for serving (optional)

Hot sauce, for serving (optional)

Tortilla chips, for serving (optional)

GLUTEN-FREE
NUT-FREE
SOY-FREE
VEGAN

PREP TIME
10 minutes

COOK TIME
8 to 10 hours on low /
4 to 6 hours on high

TOTAL TIME
8 to 10 hours, 10 minutes

Ingredient Tip: You can use 2 (14.5-ounce) cans of diced tomatoes instead of fresh, which will save you the bother of chopping the fresh tomatoes. And, if you don't have cooked beans ready, use 2 (15-ounce) cans of black beans instead.

While this recipe is gluten-free, check your spice labels. Some contain wheat, rye, or barley.

1. Coat a 4-quart slow cooker insert with cooking spray.

2. In the prepared cooker, combine the black beans, tomatoes, onion, green bell pepper, lentils, vegetable broth, chili powder, cumin, garlic, black pepper, salt, and cayenne. Stir to combine.

3. Cover the slow cooker and cook on low heat for 8 to 10 hours (recommended), or on high heat for 4 to 6 hours.

Continued

4. Serve immediately with sliced avocado, hot sauce, or tortilla chips (if using), or transfer the chili to an airtight container and refrigerate overnight to develop the flavors. To serve, reheat in a saucepan over medium heat until warm.

5. The chili can be refrigerated in an airtight container for up to 5 days or frozen for up to 6 months.

Per Serving: Calories: 321; Total Fat: 2g; Sodium: 332mg; Sugars: 5g; Carbohydrates: 57g; Fiber: 25g; Protein: 22g

MUTTER DAL CURRY *Serves 4*

A hearty Indian dish of peas and lentils, this is one of my all-time favorites to order out, along with *mutter paneer*, which has cubes of the beloved Indian non-melting cheese instead of lentils. Add some paneer cubes 15 minutes before the end of cooking and you'll have the best of both worlds. The creaminess of the dal and the crunch of the fresh peas are exceptional alongside the rich, earthy Indian spices.

½ cup dried lentils

2 cups Vegetable Scrap Broth (page 14) or store-bought broth

1 (14.5-ounce) can diced tomatoes

1 onion, chopped

2½ tablespoons garam masala

2 tablespoons ground fenugreek

2 tablespoons minced garlic

1 tablespoon ginger paste

1 tablespoon ground coriander

2 teaspoons ground cumin

1 teaspoon ground turmeric

2 cups peas

½ cup heavy (whipping) cream

½ cup Yogurt (page 20) or store-bought plain yogurt

2 tablespoons ghee

Cooked Rice (page 17) or cauliflower rice, for serving (optional)

GLUTEN-FREE
NUT-FREE
SOY-FREE

PREP TIME
15 minutes

COOK TIME
8 hours

TOTAL TIME
8 hours, 15 minutes

Per Serving: Calories: 394; Total Fat: 20g; Sodium: 61mg; Sugars: 12g; Carbohydrates: 42g; Fiber: 15g; Protein: 15g

1. In a 4-quart slow cooker, stir together the lentils and vegetable broth.

2. In a blender, combine the tomatoes, onion, garam masala, fenugreek, garlic, ginger paste, coriander, cumin, and turmeric. Blend until smooth. Add the mixture to the slow cooker.

3. Cover the slow cooker and cook on low heat for 8 hours.

4. Stir in the peas, heavy cream, yogurt, and ghee. Re-cover the cooker and cook on high heat for 15 minutes more.

5. Serve the curry over rice or cauliflower rice (if using).

MASSAMAN CURRY *Serves 4*

My first true love of curries started here. This is a relatively mild yellow curry, often paired with potatoes, cashews, and avocados in Thai cuisine. I usually make it spicy by adding chili oil or asking them to make my dish "Thai spicy" if I'm at a restaurant, but if you prefer it mild, leave the recipe as is. You can also swap out the mushrooms for whatever proteins you prefer, like chickpeas or lentils, or use mixed vegetables.

1 tablespoon olive oil

8 ounces portobello mushrooms, cut into slices

½ cup Vegetable Scrap Broth (page 14) or store-bought broth, plus more as needed

½ cup coconut milk

1 tablespoon massaman curry paste

1 tablespoon sugar

¾ teaspoon salt

1 cup chopped onion

1 cup cubed potato

4 cardamom pods

1 cinnamon stick (optional)

2 bay leaves (optional)

2 cups cooked Rice (page 17), for serving

¼ cup cashews, for garnish

½ avocado, diced, for garnish

Chopped fresh cilantro or Thai basil, for garnish

Chili oil, for garnish

GLUTEN-FREE
SOY-FREE
VEGAN

PREP TIME
5 minutes

COOK TIME
8 hours

TOTAL TIME
8 hours, 5 minutes

Ingredient Tip: Massaman curry paste can be found at Asian markets or in the international section of your grocery store. Be sure to read the ingredients on the label, as many types of massaman curry paste include shrimp or fish sauce and are not vegetarian.

1. In a 4-quart slow cooker, stir together the olive oil, mushrooms, and vegetable broth.

2. In a small bowl, stir together the coconut milk, curry paste, sugar, and salt. Set aside.

3. Add the onion and potato to the slow cooker. Wrap the cardamom pods, cinnamon stick (if using), and bay leaves (if using) in cheesecloth and add the sachet to the slow cooker. If you don't have cheesecloth, add them directly into the mixture and remove them later.

4. Pour the coconut-milk mixture over the mushrooms and vegetables and stir to combine.

5. Cover the slow cooker and cook on low heat for 8 hours, adding more broth if you prefer your curry thinner. Remove and discard the sachet or individual spices.

6. Serve the curry over rice garnished with cashews, avocado, fresh cilantro, and chili oil.

Per Serving: Calories: 384; Total Fat: 21g; Sodium: 454mg; Sugars: 7g; Carbohydrates: 46g; Fiber: 5g; Protein: 7g

CHICKPEA OR MUSHROOM CURRY *Serves 4*

Chickpeas and mushrooms are two vegetarian staples in family-friendly vegetarian meals. I like to use mushrooms in place of beef or chicken and include chickpeas in classic recipes, but these ingredients really shine on their own, particularly in Indian cuisine.

½ cup dried chickpeas **and/or** 8 ounces portobello mushrooms, cut into strips

2 cups Vegetable Scrap Broth (page 14) or store-bought broth

1 (14.5-ounce) can diced tomatoes

1 onion, chopped

2½ tablespoons garam masala

2 tablespoons ground fenugreek

2 tablespoons minced garlic

1 tablespoon ginger paste

1 tablespoon ground coriander

2 teaspoons ground cumin

1 teaspoon ground turmeric

½ cup heavy (whipping) cream

2 tablespoons ghee

½ cup Yogurt (page 20) or store-bought plain yogurt

2 cups frozen peas

Cooked Rice (page 17) or cauliflower rice, for serving (optional)

GLUTEN-FREE
NUT-FREE
SOY-FREE

PREP TIME
15 minutes

COOK TIME
8 hours

TOTAL TIME
8 hours, 15 minutes

Per Serving: Calories: 382; Total Fat: 22g; Sodium: 77mg; Sugars: 12g; Carbohydrates: 39g; Fiber: 11g; Protein: 12g

1. In a 4-quart slow cooker, combine the chickpeas (and/or mushrooms) and vegetable broth.

2. In a blender, combine the tomatoes, onion, garam masala, fenugreek, garlic, ginger paste, coriander, cumin, and turmeric and blend until smooth. Add the sauce to the slow cooker.

3. Cover the slow cooker and cook on low heat for 8 hours.

4. Stir in the heavy cream, ghee, yogurt, and peas. Re-cover the cooker and cook for 15 minutes more.

5. Serve over rice or cauliflower rice (if using).

CHICKPEA KORMA *Serves 4*

Korma is a good beginner Indian dish for those who don't typically enjoy spicy foods. By some accounts, it was created in Britain rather than India, much like butter chicken. If you'd like it spicier, add some chili oil or cayenne pepper.

2 cups Vegetable Scrap Broth (page 14) or store-bought broth

1 (14.5-ounce) can diced tomatoes, with juice

1 cup dried chickpeas

½ cup almond butter

1 large potato, peeled and cut into ½-inch chunks

1 large onion, chopped

1 yellow bell pepper, seeded and chopped

1 garlic clove, minced

1 teaspoon salt

1 teaspoon curry powder

½ teaspoon ground cloves

1 cinnamon stick

½ cup Yogurt (page 20) or store-bought plain yogurt

2 cups cooked Rice (page 17), for serving

GLUTEN-FREE
SOY-FREE

PREP TIME
5 minutes

COOK TIME
8 hours

TOTAL TIME
8 hours, 5 minutes

1. In a 4-quart slow cooker, stir together the vegetable broth, tomatoes and juice, chickpeas, almond butter, potato, onion, yellow bell pepper, garlic, salt, curry powder, cloves, and cinnamon stick.

2. Cover the slow cooker and cook on low heat for 6 to 8 hours.

3. Remove and discard the cinnamon stick. Stir in the yogurt. Serve the korma over rice.

Per Serving: Calories: 458; Total Fat: 6g; Sodium: 520mg; Sugars: 15g; Carbohydrates: 87g; Fiber: 14g; Protein: 18g

5

MAIN DISHES

BLACK BEAN–AVOCADO FRITTATA *Serves 4*

Frittatas are one of the true joys of breakfast. Much like quesadillas or fried rice, you can throw leftovers of just about any variety into a frittata and come up with a delicious meal. What I've given you here is a great starting point.

1 tablespoon olive oil

8 large eggs

¼ cup milk

1 teaspoon salt

1 cup cooked black beans (see Slow-Cooked Beans, page 15)

1 cup shredded Cheddar cheese

½ cup Caramelized Onions (page 42)

½ cup Tomatillo Salsa (page 47)

2 avocados, peeled, pitted, and sliced

Chopped fresh cilantro, for garnish (optional)

Diced jalapeño pepper, for garnish (optional)

Sour cream, for serving

GLUTEN-FREE
NUT-FREE
SOY-FREE

PREP TIME
15 minutes

COOK TIME
3 hours, 5 minutes

TOTAL TIME
3 hours, 20 minutes

Variation Tip: The frittata will fill 8 corn tortillas to make really great breakfast tacos.

1. Rub the olive oil inside a 4-quart slow cooker insert.

2. In a large bowl, whisk the eggs, milk, and salt. Pour the mixture into the prepared slow cooker.

3. Add the black beans, Cheddar cheese, onions, and salsa and gently stir to combine.

4. Cover the slow cooker and cook on low heat for 3 hours.

5. Add the avocado, cilantro, and jalapeño (if using). Re-cover the cooker and cook on high heat for 5 minutes more.

6. Cut the frittata into slices and serve with sour cream on the side.

Per Serving: Calories: 510; Total Fat: 37g; Sodium: 612mg; Sugars: 4g; Carbohydrates: 23g; Fiber: 11g; Protein: 26g

SHAKSHUKA *Serves 6*

Shakshuka is one of those frugal culinary delights that, if you didn't grow up with it, might not be on your radar. It's a humble dish of eggs baked in a chunky tomato sauce and, though it originated in Africa, is often found in Mediterranean and Middle Eastern cuisines. If you're in a hurry, use your favorite marinara or the Lentil Bolognese/Marinara (page 136).

2 pounds Roma tomatoes, diced

3 tablespoons olive oil

1 tablespoon minced garlic

1 tablespoon ground cumin

1 teaspoon salt

½ cup boiling water

6 large eggs

Salt

Freshly ground black pepper

Bread or rice, for serving

GLUTEN-FREE
NUT-FREE
SOY-FREE

PREP TIME
10 minutes

COOK TIME
5 hours, 10 minutes

TOTAL TIME
5 hours, 20 minutes

1. In a 4-quart slow cooker, stir together the tomatoes, olive oil, garlic, cumin, salt, and boiling water.

2. Cover the slow cooker and cook on high heat for 1 hour.

3. Reduce the heat to low and cook for 4 hours more.

4. Use a spoon to create 6 shallow wells in the tomato sauce.

5. Crack an egg into each well. Re-cover the cooker and cook on high heat for 8 to 10 minutes, or until the eggs are set.

6. Season with salt and pepper and serve with bread or rice, as desired.

Per Serving: Calories: 165; Total Fat: 13g; Sodium: 467mg; Sugars: 2g; Carbohydrates: 7g; Fiber: 4g; Protein: 8g

FALAFEL *Serves 6*

I still remember fondly the first time I tried falafel in high school. This Mediterranean treat was like a dream come true for a vegetarian in the 1990s. Chickpeas and spices mixed together in a protein-packed ball that can be eaten on its own or in a sandwich with delicious sauces, lettuce, and veggies. I learned to make my own falafel when I had children and didn't get out much. This slow cooker recipe has evolved quite a bit over the years and has even prompted a spin-off recipe, Chickpea Nuggets (page 129).

2 cups dried chickpeas

½ teaspoon baking soda

1 cup chopped fresh parsley

¾ cup chopped fresh cilantro, plus more for serving

2 tablespoons minced garlic

1 tablespoon freshly ground black pepper

1 tablespoon caraway seeds

1 tablespoon ground turmeric

1 tablespoon ground coriander

1 tablespoon ground cumin

1 teaspoon salt

1 teaspoon ground allspice

1 teaspoon ground cloves

1 teaspoon dried marjoram

½ tablespoon ground cinnamon

1 large egg

½ onion, chopped

¼ cup freshly squeezed lime juice

2 tablespoons sesame seeds, toasted

2 tablespoons olive oil

Hummus (page 46), tzatziki, Yogurt (page 20), or store-bought plain yogurt, for serving

Chopped lettuce, for serving

Diced tomato, for serving

Diced red onion, for serving

Diced cucumber, for serving

GLUTEN-FREE
NUT-FREE
SOY-FREE

PREP TIME
16 hours

COOK TIME
6 to 8 hours

TOTAL TIME
24 hours

1. In a large bowl, stir together the chickpeas, baking soda, and enough water to cover by 2 inches. Let soak overnight. Drain the chickpeas and pat them dry with paper towels.

2. In a food processor, combine the parsley and cilantro and pulse a few times.

3. Add the garlic, pepper, caraway seeds, turmeric, coriander, cumin, salt, allspice, cloves, marjoram, and cinnamon and process for about 40 seconds until a smooth mixture forms.

4. Add the chickpeas, egg, onion, lime juice, and sesame seeds and pulse until the mixture comes together and is still a little chunky. Using your hands, form the mixture into 1½-inch balls. At this point you can refrigerate the falafel balls in an airtight container for up to 5 days or freeze them for up to 6 months.

5. Pour the olive oil into a 4-quart slow cooker. Add the falafel balls.

6. Wrap the lid of the slow cooker in a clean kitchen towel, place it on the slow cooker, and cook on low heat for 6 to 8 hours.

7. Serve with hummus on the side, along with lettuce, tomato, red onion, cucumber, and cilantro for garnishing.

Per Serving: Calories: 344; Total Fat: 12g; Sodium: 530mg; Sugars: 8g; Carbohydrates: 48g; Fiber: 14g; Protein: 16g

TRINITY BEET BURGERS WITH GOAT CHEESE AND ARUGULA *Serves 4*

Ireland is calling me again with these beet burgers. I discovered this amazing burger at a hotel bar restaurant in Dublin. It was crafted of a single slice of roasted golden beet, topped with puréed red beet, goat cheese rolled in ground pistachios, and arugula, which in Ireland they call "rocket." I couldn't believe how such a simple burger could taste so delicious. I was hooked.

1 tablespoon olive oil

½ teaspoon salt

¼ teaspoon garlic powder

2 large golden beets, halved

2 large red beets, halved

1 tablespoon apple cider vinegar

¼ cup water

½ cup ground pistachios

8 ounces goat cheese, quartered

8 slices Sourdough Bread (page 49)

8 ounces arugula

NIGHTSHADE-FREE
SOY-FREE

PREP TIME
10 minutes

COOK TIME
8 hours

TOTAL TIME
8 hours, 10 minutes

1. Rub the olive oil, salt, and garlic powder all over the beets.

2. In a 4-quart slow cooker, combine the vinegar and water. Add the beets.

3. Cover the slow cooker and cook on low heat for 8 hours.

4. Place the pistachios in a small bowl. Roll each piece of goat cheese in the pistachios. Set aside.

5. In a blender or food processor, purée the red beets.

6. Assemble the burgers by placing 1 golden beet half on a slice of sourdough bread. Top with some of the red beet purée, goat cheese, and arugula. Place another slice of bread on top and serve.

Per Serving: Calories: 449; Total Fat: 23g; Sodium: 504mg; Sugars: 11g; Carbohydrates: 42g; Fiber: 6g; Protein: 22g

MONGOLIAN MUSHROOMS *Serves 4*

One of the few meat-based Chinese dishes I've tried at restaurants and really enjoyed is Mongolian beef, but I always add veggies to it because I think it's kind of boring otherwise. At home, I can make it as a full-on vegetarian dish, and this version features portobello mushrooms as the star with carrots and water chestnuts along for the ride, plus the traditional sliced scallions.

1½ pounds portobello mushrooms, cut into slices

¼ cup arrowroot

1 cup grated peeled carrot

¾ cup coconut sugar

⅓ cup coconut aminos or soy sauce

6 ounces water chestnuts

2 tablespoons avocado oil

½ teaspoon minced garlic

¾ cup water

Cooked Rice (page 17), for serving (optional)

Sliced scallions, for garnish

GLUTEN-FREE
NIGHTSHADE-FREE
NUT-FREE
SOY-FREE
VEGAN

PREP TIME
10 minutes

COOK TIME
5 hours

TOTAL TIME
5 hours, 10 minutes

1. In a paper bag or glass jar, combine the mushrooms and arrowroot. Seal the bag or jar and shake to coat.

2. In a 4-quart slow cooker, combine the carrot, coconut sugar, coconut aminos, water chestnuts, avocado oil, garlic, and water. Add the mushrooms and stir until they are coated in the sauce.

3. Cover the slow cooker and cook on low heat for 4 to 5 hours.

4. Serve over rice (if using) and garnish with scallions.

Per Serving: Calories: 335; Total Fat: 8g; Sodium: 1035mg; Sugars: 41g; Carbohydrates: 65g; Fiber: 4g; Protein: 7g

MUSHROOM STROGANOFF *Serves 4*

I'm a huge fan of stroganoff, with its creamy sauce, mushrooms, and noodles. If you leave out the beef and use portobello mushrooms instead, it's perfection in my mind. I think portobellos are the "meatiest" of the mushrooms, but you could use whatever variety you like best. The combination of mushrooms and caramelized onions with the creamy sauce is absolutely delicious over rice or noodles. Serve it whichever way you prefer.

1½ pounds portobello mushrooms, cut into slices

1½ cups Vegetable Scrap Broth (page 14) or store-bought broth

½ cup Caramelized Onions (page 42)

4 tablespoons butter

1 tablespoon freshly squeezed lemon juice

1 tablespoon red wine vinegar

1 tablespoon Dijon mustard

1 teaspoon minced garlic

½ teaspoon salt

¼ teaspoon freshly ground black pepper

1 cup Yogurt (page 20), store-bought plain yogurt, or sour cream

2 tablespoons gluten-free flour

1 pound cooked gluten-free brown rice noodles, for serving

Sliced scallions, for serving

GLUTEN-FREE
NIGHTSHADE-FREE
NUT-FREE
SOY-FREE

PREP TIME
15 minutes

COOK TIME
4 hours, 15 minutes

TOTAL TIME
4 hours, 30 minutes

1. In a 4-quart slow cooker, stir together the mushrooms, vegetable broth, onions, butter, lemon juice, vinegar, mustard, garlic, salt, and pepper.

2. Cover the slow cooker and cook on low heat for 4 hours.

3. Whisk in the yogurt and flour. Re-cover the cooker and cook on high heat for 15 minutes more.

4. Serve the stroganoff over the noodles and sprinkle with scallions.

Per Serving: Calories: 381; Total Fat: 15g; Sodium: 464mg; Sugars: 8g; Carbohydrates: 53g; Fiber: 6g; Protein: 11g

MUSHROOM AND PEPPER FAJITAS *Serves 6*

Most Mexican restaurants offer vegetarian fajitas and they can be pretty tasty, but there's something about making your own that makes them extra delicious. It's also a great way to control allergens for those who have concerns.

FOR THE MARINADE

¼ cup freshly squeezed lime juice

¼ cup Taco Seasoning (page 32)

2 tablespoons avocado oil

2 tablespoons olive oil

1 teaspoon ground cumin

½ teaspoon garlic powder

Salt

Freshly ground black pepper

Chopped fresh cilantro

FOR THE VEGETABLES

1 pound portobello mushrooms, cut into slices

½ cup avocado oil

2 red bell peppers, seeded and cut into slices

2 green bell peppers, seeded and cut into slices

1 small zucchini, cut into slices

1 cup Caramelized Onions (page 42)

3 garlic cloves, minced

2 tablespoons Taco Seasoning (page 32)

Salt

Mexican rice (see Rice, page 17, Variation Tip), for serving

Black beans (see Slow-Cooked Beans, page 15), for serving

GLUTEN-FREE
NUT-FREE
SOY-FREE
VEGAN

PREP TIME
8 hours

COOK TIME
4 to 6 hours

TOTAL TIME
14 hours

To make the marinade
In a large bowl, stir together the lime juice, taco seasoning, avocado oil, olive oil, cumin, and garlic powder and season with salt, pepper, and cilantro.

Continued

To make the vegetables

1. Add the mushrooms to the marinade. Stir to coat, cover the bowl, and refrigerate for 8 hours or up to overnight.

2. In a 4-quart slow cooker, stir together the marinated mushrooms, avocado oil, red and green bell peppers, zucchini, onions, garlic, and taco seasoning. Season with salt.

3. Cover the slow cooker and cook on low heat for 4 to 6 hours.

4. Serve with Mexican rice and black beans.

Per Serving: Calories: 377; Total Fat: 19g; Sodium: 226mg; Sugars: 6g; Carbohydrates: 45g; Fiber: 6g; Protein: 8g

MUSHROOM BREAD PUDDING CUPS *Serves 8*

Bread puddings are classic comfort foods and I like savory versions like this one, as well as sweet desserts like the Blueberry-Lemon Bread Pudding (page 155) and the Sticky Toffee Bread Pudding (page 156). Portobello mushrooms and shallots are the stars here, with backup notes from parsley and Parmesan. These are quite elegant when baked in little 8-ounce ramekins, but you can also cook it in a 1½-quart baking dish, if you don't have ramekins.

2 tablespoons butter, plus more to coat the ramekins

1½ pounds portobello mushrooms, diced

½ cup finely chopped shallot

½ teaspoon salt, plus more for seasoning

Freshly ground black pepper

½ cup finely chopped fresh flat-leaf parsley

1 teaspoon minced garlic

1 cup heavy (whipping) cream

1 cup milk

4 large eggs

½ cup grated Parmesan cheese

4 cups (½-inch) Sourdough Bread (page 49) cubes

NIGHTSHADE-FREE
NUT-FREE
SOY-FREE

PREP TIME
30 minutes

COOK TIME
4 hours

TOTAL TIME
4 hours, 30 minutes

Variation Tip: You can also cook this dish in a 1½-quart baking dish. Check to make sure the center is set at 4 hours, adding more cooking time, if needed.

1. In a saucepan over medium heat, melt the butter. Add the mushrooms and shallot and cook for about 10 minutes, until the shallot is translucent.

2. Season with salt and pepper and continue to cook, stirring occasionally, for 15 minutes more.

3. Add the parsley and garlic and cook for 2 minutes. Set aside.

4. In a medium bowl, whisk the heavy cream, milk, eggs, Parmesan cheese, and ½ teaspoon of salt.

5. Coat 8 (8-ounce) ramekins with butter.

Continued

6. Divide the bread cubes and the mushroom mixture among the ramekins. Pour the cream mixture over the bread in each ramekin. Place the ramekins into a 6-quart slow cooker.

7. Carefully pour water into the slow cooker until it comes halfway up the sides of the ramekins.

8. Wrap the lid of the slow cooker in a clean kitchen towel, place it on the slow cooker, and cook on low heat for 4 hours. Serve hot.

Per Serving: Calories: 302; Total Fat: 19g; Sodium: 458mg; Sugars: 4g; Carbohydrates: 23g; Fiber: 2g; Protein: 12g

MOM'S PEPPER "STEAK" PORTOBELLOS   *Serves 4*

Mom made this recipe with real steak as a regular part of her rotation when I was a kid. It was one that I enjoyed even though it was meat, which was rare for me. When I had kids, I asked her for the recipe and I started making it with portobellos (though I occasionally still make it with steak for Mr. Meaty).

4 portobello mushrooms, cut into slices

2 tablespoons arrowroot

4 cups Vegetable Scrap Broth (page 14) or store-bought broth

3 cups sliced green bell pepper

1 (15-ounce) can tomato sauce

1 bay leaf

2 cups cooked Rice (page 17), for serving

GLUTEN-FREE
NUT-FREE
SOY-FREE
VEGAN

PREP TIME
10 minutes

COOK TIME
4 to 6 hours

TOTAL TIME
6 hours, 10 minutes

1. In a large bowl, toss together the mushrooms and arrowroot. Transfer to a 4-quart slow cooker.

2. Add the vegetable broth, green bell pepper, tomato sauce, and bay leaf. Gently stir to combine.

3. Cover the slow cooker and cook on low heat for 4 to 6 hours.

4. Remove and discard the bay leaf and serve the mixture over rice.

Per Serving: Calories: 222; Total Fat: 1g; Sodium: 400mg; Sugars: 16g; Carbohydrates: 50g; Fiber: 5g; Protein: 8g

NO CARNE GUISADA   *Serves 10*

Carne guisada translates to "stewed meat," so, of course, this version is the no-meat version with portobello mushrooms as the main ingredient. Tomatoes, onion, bell peppers, and Mexican spices lift the flavors of the mushrooms and the mixture is excellent served as tacos, rolled up in tortillas for burritos, or simply over rice.

2 pounds portobello mushrooms, cut into slices

Salt

Freshly ground black pepper

2 tablespoons olive oil, divided

1 yellow onion, diced

1 green bell pepper, seeded and diced

1 jalapeño pepper, seeded and finely diced

1 tablespoon minced garlic

2 cups Vegetable Scrap Broth (page 14) or store-bought broth

1 (14.5-ounce can) diced tomatoes

¼ cup gluten-free flour

1½ teaspoons ground cumin

1 teaspoon chili powder

1 teaspoon dried oregano

2 bay leaves

Tortillas, for serving (optional)

Cooked Rice (page 17), for serving (optional)

Mashed avocado, for topping

Finely diced red onion, for topping

Tomatillo Salsa (page 47), for topping

Chopped fresh cilantro, for topping

NUT-FREE
SOY-FREE
VEGAN

PREP TIME
15 minutes

COOK TIME
4 to 6 hours

TOTAL TIME
6 hours, 15 minutes

1. Season the mushrooms with salt and pepper and place them in a 6-quart slow cooker with 1 tablespoon of olive oil.

2. In a large skillet over medium heat, heat the remaining 1 tablespoon of oil. Add the onion, green bell pepper, jalapeño, and garlic. Cook for about 5 minutes, until the onion is translucent. Transfer the vegetables to the slow cooker.

3. Add the vegetable broth, tomatoes, flour, cumin, chili powder, oregano, and bay leaves and stir to combine.

4. Cover the slow cooker and cook on low heat for 4 to 6 hours. Remove and discard the bay leaves.

5. Serve the guisada in tortillas or with rice, as desired, and top with avocado, red onion, tomatillo salsa, and fresh cilantro.

Per Serving: Calories: 205; Total Fat: 8g; Sodium: 231mg; Sugars: 4g; Carbohydrates: 27g; Fiber: 4g; Protein: 6g

ENCHILADAS NOPALITOS *Serves 8*

Nopales are prickly pear cactus and I absolutely love them. I discovered them at a yummy Mexican restaurant near my mother's house and now I can't imagine what I've done without them all my life. Delicious! The kids thought my original version was a bit too spicy, so I have since nixed the jalapeños for them but add them separately to Mr. Meaty's and my own enchiladas. Yep, that's how we adult. Jalapeño style.

2 cups jarred nopalitos pieces

1 cup Enchilada Sauce (page 31)

2 tomatoes, chopped

1 red onion, chopped

1 yellow onion, chopped

1 head garlic, peeled and chopped

1 jalapeño pepper, sliced (optional)

1 cup chopped fresh spinach

Salt

8 corn tortillas

Shredded Cheddar cheese or vegan cheese, for serving

Chopped fresh cilantro, for serving (optional)

GLUTEN-FREE
NUT-FREE
SOY-FREE

PREP TIME
10 minutes

COOK TIME
8 hours

TOTAL TIME
8 hours, 10 minutes

Ingredient Tip: Nopalitos can be found in jars in the Mexican foods section of your grocery store.

1. In a 4-quart slow cooker, stir together the nopalitos, enchilada sauce, tomatoes, red onion, yellow onion, garlic, jalapeño (if using), and spinach. Season with salt.

2. Cover the slow cooker and cook on low heat for 8 hours.

3. Place spoonfuls of the nopalitos filling into the tortillas and top with the Cheddar cheese and cilantro (if using).

Per Serving: Calories: 134; Total Fat: 3g; Sodium: 297mg; Sugars: 3g; Carbohydrates: 23g; Fiber: 2g; Protein: 4g

CURRY BAKED POTATO BALLS   *Serves 4*

Also known as *malai kofta*, these Indian dumplings are filled with spices such as cilantro and turmeric and are often on menus at Indian restaurants. They are served with an orange-hued curry sauce made primarily with peppers, tomatoes, yogurt, and spices.

FOR THE KOFTA

1 pound baked Yukon gold potatoes

2 tablespoons finely chopped red onion

2 tablespoons finely chopped fresh cilantro

1 teaspoon chili powder

½ teaspoon ground turmeric

½ teaspoon salt

FOR THE CURRY

6 garlic cloves, minced

2 tablespoons tomato paste

1 teaspoon chili powder

1 teaspoon ground coriander

¼ teaspoon cayenne pepper

¼ teaspoon salt

1¼ cups water

2 tablespoons olive oil

2 red onions, finely chopped

2 tablespoons Yogurt (page 20) or store-boughtplainyogurt

¼ cup chopped fresh cilantro

2 cups cooked Rice (page 17), for serving

GLUTEN-FREE
NUT-FREE
SOY-FREE

PREP TIME
20 minutes

COOK TIME
8 hours

TOTAL TIME
8 hours, 20 minutes

To make the kofta

1. In a large bowl, using a potato masher, mash the potatoes.

2. Add the red onion, cilantro, chili powder, turmeric, and salt and mix to thoroughly combine. Using your hands, a melon baller, or a cookie scoop, form the mixture into 1-inch balls. Set aside.

To make the curry

1. In a small bowl, stir together the garlic, tomato paste, chili powder, coriander, cayenne, salt, and water. Set aside.

Continued

2. In a large skillet over medium-high heat, warm the olive oil. Add the red onions and cook for about 15 minutes, until they are translucent and start to brown. Transfer to a 4-quart slow cooker and stir in the curry sauce.

3. Place the koftas on top of the curry.

4. Cover the slow cooker and cook on low heat for 8 hours, until the koftas are baked through and browned. Transfer the koftas to a bowl and set aside.

5. Stir the yogurt into the curry in the slow cooker. Transfer the curry to a serving bowl, top with the koftas, and sprinkle with cilantro. Serve with rice.

Per Serving: Calories: 306; Total Fat: 8g; Sodium: 475mg; Sugars: 5g; Carbohydrates: 54g; Fiber: 5g; Protein: 6g

BUILD YOUR OWN TACOS BAR   *Serves 4*

When we are in a hurry, this is our go-to Taco Tuesday extravaganza buffet dish. It's the perfect solution for a blended-eater family: Set out multiple proteins and toppings and everyone gets to pick what they want. The key is to have ingredients such as beans and rice already cooked and waiting in the refrigerator. Toppings can be quickly chopped up or shredded. All you need to do is heat things up and you're good to go.

1 cup cooked chickpeas (see Slow-Cooked Beans, page 15)

1 cup cooked black beans (see Slow-Cooked Beans, page 15)

1 cup cooked Rice (page 17)

1 cup diced avocado

1 cup shredded Cheddar cheese

½ cup Tomatillo Salsa (page 47)

4 ounces pitted olives, sliced

1 cup Yogurt (page 20), store-bought plain yogurt, or sour cream

Shredded lettuce, for serving

Mexican hot sauce, for serving

Taco shells or tortillas, for serving

NUT-FREE
SOY-FREE

PREP TIME
15 minutes

TOTAL TIME
15 minutes

1. Place each ingredient in a separate bowl, buffet style, on the dinner table or kitchen counter and let everyone put together their own tacos or burritos however they like.

2. Eat. Repeat.

Per Serving: Calories: 529; Total Fat: 25g; Sodium: 566mg; Sugars: 7g; Carbohydrates: 58g; Fiber: 14g; Protein: 21g

BUILD YOUR OWN LOADED
BAKED POTATOES *Serves 4*

Another favorite buffet-style meal in our family lets everyone add whatever toppings they like to steaming-hot baked potatoes. This recipe is also great for using leftovers and a fabulous way to satisfy different eating styles. Vegetarians and meat eaters alike will enjoy a hearty meal without compromise. Try topping these with Black Bean–Lentil Chili (page 85), Real Food Mac and Cheese Sauce (page 25), or Mongolian Mushrooms (page 99) if you have them in the refrigerator. Don't limit yourself to what I've shown here. Add meat proteins or other vegetables for those who want them.

4 russet potatoes

Olive oil

Salt

Chopped cooked broccoli, for topping

Butter, for topping

Real Food Mac and Cheese Sauce (page 25), for topping

Black Bean Lentil Chili (page 85), for topping

Chopped fresh chives, for topping

Garlic powder, for topping

Hot sauce, for topping

Diced jalapeño pepper, for topping

Sour cream, for topping

Freshly ground black pepper

GLUTEN-FREE
NUT-FREE
SOY-FREE

PREP TIME
15 minutes

COOK TIME
8 hours

TOTAL TIME
8 hours, 15 minutes

Per Serving (toppings excluded): Calories: 178; Total Fat: 1g; Sodium: 158mg; Sugars: 1g; Carbohydrates: 39g; Fiber: 3g; Protein: 5g

1. Poke the potatoes with a fork several times, rub them with olive oil, and sprinkle with salt. Place the potatoes in a 4-quart slow cooker.

2. Cover the slow cooker and cook on high heat for 5 hours or on low heat for 8 hours, until the potatoes are tender.

3. Place each topping, as desired, in a separate bowl on the table or kitchen counter, buffet style, and let everyone put together their own fully loaded potatoes.

4. Eat. Repeat.

BUILD YOUR OWN SUSHI BOWLS *Serves 4*

Sushi bowls are a relatively new feature in our dinnertime rotation. We started adding them on Salad/Rice Bowl Wednesdays and it's another great buffet option for blended eaters. In addition to the vegetarian options shown, we often serve smoked salmon. If you're a pescatarian or omnivore, feel free to add that to your buffet.

FOR THE PICKLED CUCUMBER

2 tablespoons sugar

2 tablespoons rice vinegar

1 cucumber, cut into slices

FOR THE SAUTÉED MUSHROOMS

1 tablespoon olive oil

⅔ cup mushrooms

FOR THE SUSHI BOWLS

¼ cup shredded peeled carrot

½ cup diced avocado

½ cup shelled edamame

½ cup bean sprouts

6 cups cooked sushi rice (see Rice, page 17, Variation Tip)

Black and white sesame seeds, for garnish

4 ounces cream cheese, diced (optional)

Soy sauce, or coconut aminos, for serving

Gochujang, for serving

GLUTEN-FREE
NUT-FREE

PREP TIME
1 hour

COOK TIME
10 minutes

TOTAL TIME
30 minutes

Ingredient Tip: Gochujang is a Korean chile paste that is a mix of sweet, savory, and spicy. Add a spoonful to give your dish a little extra flavor. You can find it in the Asian section of your grocery store.

To make the pickled cucumber
In a medium bowl, stir together the sugar and vinegar until the sugar dissolves. Add the cucumber, cover, and refrigerate for at least 1 hour.

Continued

To make the sautéed mushrooms

In a small skillet over medium heat, heat the olive oil. Add the mushrooms and cook for 5 to 6 minutes, stirring occasionally, until tender. Set aside.

To make the sushi bowls

1. Place the prepared ingredients, including the pickled cucumbers, sautéed mushrooms, and garnishes, in separate bowls on the table or kitchen counter and serve, buffet style, and let everyone put together their own sushi rice bowls with their toppings of choice.

2. Eat. Repeat.

Per Serving: Calories: 514; Total Fat: 10g; Sodium: 12mg; Sugars: 8g; Carbohydrates: 95g; Fiber: 4g; Protein: 11g

BIBIMBAP *Serves 4*

The joy of eating Korean food is a pleasure I discovered relatively late in life. We foster cats from a shelter in Atlanta's Koreatown and our regular trips to FurKids led to my love of bibimbap and gochujang and a deeper understanding of the subtle nuances of kimchi. Until then, I wasn't a fan of eggs in any way other than over-hard or scrambled, but I've come to enjoy a runny sunny-side up egg in bibimbap.

FOR THE VEGETABLES

4 ounces fresh spinach

4 ounces mung bean sprouts

¼ cup edamame

1 teaspoon minced scallion

1 teaspoon minced garlic

1½ teaspoons white sesame seeds, divided

1½ teaspoons black sesame seeds, divided

5 tablespoons sesame oil, divided

¾ cup julienned cucumber

4 shiitake mushrooms, cut into slices

2 small carrots, peeled and julienned

1 small zucchini, julienned

½ teaspoon salt

4 cups cooked sushi rice (see Rice, page 17, Variation Tip)

FOR THE SAUCE

4 tablespoons gochujang

2 tablespoons sesame oil

1 teaspoon minced garlic

½ teaspoon sugar

½ teaspoon rice vinegar

½ teaspoon water

FOR THE GARNISH

¼ cup coconut oil

4 large eggs

Nori seaweed, cut into strips

GLUTEN-FREE
NUT-FREE
SOY-FREE

PREP TIME
20 minutes

COOK TIME
2 hours, 45 minutes

TOTAL TIME
3 hours, 5 minutes

To make the vegetables

1. Bring a large pot of water to a boil over high heat. Add the spinach, mung bean sprouts, and edamame. Blanch for 30 seconds. Drain, transfer to a large bowl, and toss with the scallion, garlic, 1 teaspoon of white sesame seeds, 1 teaspoon of black sesame seeds, and 1 tablespoon of sesame oil.

Continued

2. In a large skillet over medium-high heat, warm the remaining 4 tablespoons of sesame oil. Add the cucumber, shiitake, carrots, and zucchini. Sauté for about 5 minutes, until crisp-tender. Add the salt, the remaining ½ teaspoon of white sesame seeds, and the remaining ½ teaspoon of black sesame seeds and toss to combine.

To make the sauce
In a small bowl, whisk the gochujang, sesame oil, garlic, sugar, vinegar, and water. Set aside.

To make the garnish
In a skillet over medium heat, warm the coconut oil. Add the eggs and cook them, sunny-side-up, to your desired doneness.

To assemble the bibimbap
1. Using about half the sauce, pour a little in the bottom of each of 4 bowls and top each with rice.

2. Arrange the blanched spinach, mung bean sprouts, edamame, sautéed cucumber, shiitake, carrots, and zucchini on top of the rice.

3. Center a fried egg on top of each bowl and add strips of nori seaweed on top. Serve with the remaining sauce on the side.

Per Serving: Calories: 795; Total Fat: 41g; Sodium: 986mg; Sugars: 14g; Carbohydrates: 91g; Fiber: 5g; Protein: 22g

SPICY RICE BALLS *Serves 8*

This savory treat is a mix of rice and oats that we often eat as a main dish, dipped in sauce like the marinara version of Lentil Bolognese/Marinara (page 136).

½ cup quick-cooking oatmeal

¼ cup milk

2 cups cooked white Rice (page 17)

1¼ cups diced onion

¾ cup almond flour

1 teaspoon salt

1 teaspoon dried basil

½ teaspoon dried oregano

¼ teaspoon cayenne pepper (optional)

2 large eggs

2 cups Lentil Bolognese/Marinara (page 136)

GLUTEN-FREE
SOY-FREE

PREP TIME
20 minutes

COOK TIME
4 to 8 hours

TOTAL TIME
8 hours, 20 minutes

1. In a small bowl, stir together the oatmeal and milk. Let sit for 5 minutes.

2. In a large bowl, stir together the cooked rice, onion, almond flour, salt, basil, oregano, and cayenne (if using).

3. Add the oatmeal mixture to the rice mixture and stir to combine.

4. Add the eggs and mix to combine. Using your hands, form the mixture into 1½-inch balls and set aside.

5. Pour the marinara into a 4-quart slow cooker. Place the rice balls on top of the sauce.

6. Cover the slow cooker and cook on low heat for 4 to 8 hours, or until golden brown.

7. If you'd like the rice balls to be brown and crispy, place the crock under the broiler for a few minutes.

Per Serving: Calories: 176; Total Fat: 5g; Sodium: 392mg; Sugars: 2g; Carbohydrates: 23g; Fiber: 2g; Protein: 5g

CHICKPEA-BROCCOLI RICE *Serves 8*

Modeled after chicken-broccoli rice casserole, this homey classic is a conversion of a family-friendly recipe that's great for potlucks and meal trains.

4 cups broccoli florets

2½ cups brown rice

2 cups cooked chickpeas (see Slow-Cooked Beans, page 15)

2 cups milk

1½ cups Vegetable Scrap Broth (page 14) or store-bought broth

1 cup diced mushrooms

⅔ cup diced yellow onion

4 garlic cloves, minced

8 tablespoons (1 stick) butter

½ cup gluten-free flour

2 cups shredded Cheddar cheese

Salt

Freshly ground black pepper

GLUTEN-FREE
NIGHTSHADE-FREE
NUT-FREE
SOY-FREE

PREP TIME
20 minutes

COOK TIME
3 hours, 15 minutes

TOTAL TIME
3 hours, 35 minutes

1. In a 6-quart slow cooker, stir together the broccoli, brown rice, chickpeas, milk, vegetable broth, mushrooms, onion, garlic, butter, and flour.

2. Cover the slow cooker and cook on low heat for 2½ to 3 hours, or until the rice is tender.

3. Add the Cheddar cheese. Season with salt and pepper. Re-cover the cooker and cook on high for 15 minutes more. Serve hot.

Per Serving: Calories: 578; Total Fat: 25g; Sodium: 307mg; Sugars: 6g; Carbohydrates: 70g; Fiber: 7g; Protein: 20g

CHICKPEA SHAWARMA RICE BOWL *Serves 4*

Chicken shawarma is a Mediterranean specialty of spiced chicken served with tabbouleh, rice, hummus, yogurt or tzatziki, red onion, lettuce, and lime slices. Here, I'm sharing my vegetarian chickpea version as a rice bowl, but you can also serve the shawarma in lettuce wraps or pita bread.

FOR THE CHICKPEA SHAWARMA

3 cups Vegetable Scrap Broth (page 14) or store-bought broth

1½ cups dried chickpeas

¼ cup olive oil

1 tablespoon ground coriander

1 tablespoon ground cumin

1 tablespoon ground cardamom

1 tablespoon freshly squeezed lime juice

1 teaspoon minced garlic

1 teaspoon paprika

½ teaspoon cayenne pepper (optional)

½ teaspoon salt

1 cup cooked Rice (page 17)

Hummus (page 46), for serving

Yogurt (page 20) or store-bought plain yogurt, for serving

Chopped red onion, for serving

Shredded lettuce, for serving

Lime slices, for serving

FOR THE TABBOULEH HERBS

10 scallions, thinly sliced

2 cups chopped fresh curly parsley

1 cup diced tomato

¼ cup chopped fresh mint

¼ cup freshly squeezed lime juice

¼ cup olive oil

Salt

Freshly ground black pepper

GLUTEN-FREE
NUT-FREE
SOY-FREE

PREP TIME
15 minutes

COOK TIME
8 hours

TOTAL TIME
8 hours, 15 minutes

Continued

To make the chickpea shawarma

1. In a 4-quart slow cooker, stir together the vegetable broth, chickpeas, olive oil, coriander, cumin, cardamom, lime juice, garlic, paprika, cayenne (if using), and salt.

2. Cover the slow cooker and cook on low heat for 8 hours.

To make the tabbouleh herbs

1. In a large bowl, stir together the scallions, parsley, tomato, mint, lime juice, and olive oil and season with salt and pepper.

2. Spoon rice into bowls and top with the chickpea shawarma, hummus, yogurt, and some of the herb mix. Serve with red onion, shredded lettuce, and lime slices on the side.

Per Serving: Calories: 685; Total Fat: 34g; Sodium: 504mg; Sugars: 17g; Carbohydrates: 79g; Fiber: 19g; Protein: 23g

BROWN RICE RISOTTO WITH FRESH PEAS, MUSHROOMS, BROCCOLI, OR CORN *Serves 8*

Rich and creamy, this vegetarian risotto is a wonderful base for adding any number of vegetables. I particularly love using fresh peas, but portobello mushrooms, broccoli, and corn are also good choices. Risotto is one of those dishes that's pretty hands-on if you make it on the stovetop, but not with the slow cooker—it's truly set it and forget it.

1 tablespoon olive oil

1½ cups brown rice

1 teaspoon minced onion flakes

3 cups Vegetable Scrap Broth (page 14) or store-bought broth

12 ounces vegetables (such as fresh peas, sautéed mushrooms, fresh corn, or finely chopped broccoli florets)

1 tablespoon minced garlic

1 teaspoon salt

½ teaspoon freshly ground black pepper

¼ teaspoon cayenne pepper (optional)

1 tablespoon butter, diced

¼ cup whole milk

1 cup shredded mozzarella cheese

2 tablespoons crushed cashews (optional)

GLUTEN-FREE
SOY-FREE

PREP TIME
10 minutes

COOK TIME
2 hours

TOTAL TIME
2 hours, 10 minutes

Variation Tip: To make this recipe vegan, substitute margarine, dairy-free milk, and dairy-free cheese in the same amounts as written.

1. In a 4-quart slow cooker, stir together the olive oil, brown rice, and onion flakes.

2. Add the vegetable broth, vegetables, garlic, salt, black pepper, and cayenne (if using) and stir to combine.

3. Scatter the butter cubes over the top.

Continued

4. Cover the slow cooker and cook on high heat for about 2 hours, checking every 45 minutes, until the liquid is absorbed and the rice is tender but not mushy. (Mine is usually done in about 1½ hours, but times may vary.)

5. Turn off the slow cooker and stir in the milk and mozzarella cheese, stirring to combine and melt the cheese.

6. Serve garnished with crushed cashews (if using).

Per Serving: Calories: 222; Total Fat: 7g; Sodium: 417mg; Sugars: 3g; Carbohydrates: 33g; Fiber: 2g; Protein: 8g

CHEESE "BURGER" CAULIFLOWER *Serves 8*

Cheeseburger and rice casseroles are a classic stovetop dinner. This variation uses cauliflower in place of the rice and lentils in place of the hamburger (and, of course, a slow cooker) resulting in a similar, yet unique, vegetarian dish. The dry mustard and garlic powder lend nice flavor to the dish, so don't be shy about increasing the amount of spices if you like even more intense flavor. Broiling the cauliflower and cheese mixture after cooking in the slow cooker will also bring out the vegetable's natural sugars, enhancing the flavor even more.

6 cups cauliflower florets

3 cups Slow-Cooked Lentils (page 16)

1 cup Vegetable Scrap Broth (page 14) or store-bought broth

1 teaspoon garlic powder

½ teaspoon dry mustard

⅛ teaspoon salt

⅛ teaspoon freshly ground black pepper

2 cups shredded Cheddar cheese

GLUTEN-FREE
NIGHTSHADE-FREE
NUT-FREE
SOY-FREE

PREP TIME
10 minutes

COOK TIME
4 hours, 15 minutes

TOTAL TIME
4 hours, 25 minutes

1. In a 4-quart slow cooker, stir together the cauliflower, cooked lentils, vegetable broth, garlic powder, dry mustard, salt, and pepper.

2. Cover the slow cooker and cook on low heat for 4 hours.

3. Add the Cheddar cheese, turn the heat to high, and re-cover the cooker. Cook for 15 minutes more until the cheese melts.

4. To brown the top, place the crock under the broiler for a few minutes before serving.

Per Serving: Calories: 223; Total Fat: 10g; Sodium: 233mg; Sugars: 4g; Carbohydrates: 20g; Fiber: 8g; Protein: 15g

CHEESY MOROCCAN ROASTED CAULIFLOWER QUINOA *Serves 4*

Moroccan spices—such as turmeric, cumin, and paprika—give this dish incredible flavor and your kitchen will smell really good.

1¾ cups Vegetable Scrap Broth (page 14) or store-bought broth

2 cups chopped cauliflower florets

1 cup quinoa, rinsed well and drained

1½ cups shredded Cheddar cheese

1 tablespoon ground turmeric

2 tablespoons ground cumin

2 tablespoons paprika (optional)

Salt

1 scallion, sliced thin (optional)

GLUTEN-FREE
NUT-FREE
SOY-FREE

PREP TIME
10 minutes

COOK TIME
4 hours, 15 minutes

TOTAL TIME
4 hours, 25 minutes

1. In a 4-quart slow cooker, stir together the vegetable broth, cauliflower, and quinoa.

2. Cover the slow cooker and cook on low heat for 3 to 4 hours.

3. Stir in the Cheddar cheese, turmeric, cumin, paprika (if using) and season with salt. Re-cover the cooker and cook on high heat for 15 minutes more.

4. Serve in bowls topped with scallion (if using).

Per Serving: Calories: 361; Total Fat: 18g; Sodium: 295mg; Sugars: 3g; Carbohydrates: 34g; Fiber: 5g; Protein: 18g

CASHEW AND PANEER KOFTA   *Serves 6*

I discovered this variety of kofta at a little Indian restaurant near my mom's house in Kansas City, Missouri, and it has the sauce of my dreams. I have attempted to replicate it and I hope I've at least gotten close. Coconut and potatoes join the cashews as the main ingredients here.

FOR THE KOFTA

1 cup paneer

1 pound boiled potatoes

⅔ cup cashews

½ cup gluten-free bread cubes

½ cup shredded unsweetened coconut

Handful fresh cilantro leaves, finely chopped

1 or 2 green chiles, finely chopped

1½ teaspoons salt

FOR THE CURRY

1 (14.5-ounce) can crushed tomatoes

½ onion, coarsely chopped

½ cup chopped fresh cilantro

½ cup coconut milk

1 tablespoon minced garlic

1 teaspoon garam masala

Salt

Freshly ground black pepper

3 cups cooked Rice (page 17), for serving

GLUTEN-FREE
SOY-FREE

PREP TIME
20 minutes

COOK TIME
8 hours

TOTAL TIME
8 hours, 20 minutes

To make the kofta

1. Grate the paneer and boiled potatoes into a large bowl. Set aside.

2. In a food processor, finely chop the cashews. Add the bread cubes and pulse once. Transfer the bread and cashews to the potato mixture and add the coconut, cilantro, green chiles, and salt. Stir to combine. Using your hands, form the mixture into 1-inch balls, compressing them slightly. Set aside.

Continued

To make the curry

1. In a food processor, combine the tomatoes, onion, cilantro, coconut milk, garlic, and garam masala and season with salt and pepper. Process until blended. Transfer the mixture to a 4-quart slow cooker.

2. Place the koftas on top of the curry.

3. Cover the slow cooker and cook on low heat for 8 hours.

4. Serve the kofta and curry over rice.

Per Serving: Calories: 442; Total Fat: 18g; Sodium: 854mg; Sugars: 9g; Carbohydrates: 62g; Fiber: 7g; Protein: 11g

CASHEW CHICKPEAS *Serves 4*

Uncle John always ordered cashew chicken at Chinese restaurants. It looked delicious! (I'm allergic to celery, so I couldn't try it.) The relative lack of vegetables in the dish seemed odd to me, though. So, when I made my own version with chickpeas, I added some extra veggies, too.

3 cups Vegetable Scrap Broth (page 14) or store-bought broth

1½ cups dried chickpeas

8 ounces sliced water chestnuts

1 green bell pepper, seeded and diced

1 large carrot, peeled and diced

1 cup Caramelized Onions (page 42)

1 tablespoon sesame oil

¼ cup coconut aminos or soy sauce

3 tablespoons maple syrup or honey

2 tablespoons rice vinegar

½ teaspoon sriracha (optional)

2 tablespoons arrowroot

2 tablespoons water

½ cup roasted cashews

2 cups broccoli florets

6 cups cooked Rice (page 17)

4 scallions, sliced

GLUTEN-FREE
SOY-FREE
VEGAN

PREP TIME
10 minutes

COOK TIME
8 hours, 15 minutes

TOTAL TIME
8 hours, 25 minutes

Per Serving: Calories: 949; Total Fat: 17g; Sodium: 95mg; Sugars: 24g; Carbohydrates: 177g; Fiber: 18g; Protein: 28g

1. In a 4-quart slow cooker, stir together the vegetable broth, chickpeas, water chestnuts, green bell pepper, carrot, onions, and sesame oil.

2. In a small bowl, whisk the coconut aminos, maple syrup, vinegar, and sriracha (if using). In another small bowl, whisk the arrowroot and water to make a slurry. Add both mixtures and the cashews to the slow cooker and stir to combine.

3. Cover the slow cooker and cook on low heat for 8 hours.

4. Add the broccoli, re-cover the cooker, and cook on high heat for 15 minutes more.

5. Spoon the cashew chickpeas into bowls over rice and top with scallions.

SPICY BUFFALO CHICKPEA OR JACKFRUIT LETTUCE WRAPS *Serves 8*

You get your choice in these yummy lettuce wraps. You can go for the chickpeas, which are delicious, or try the recipe using jackfruit, a fruit with a "meaty" texture that has taken the food world by storm in recent years. You can buy it canned and sometimes fresh in Asian markets. It's in the same family as the fig, mulberry, and breadfruit, and it's used a lot in in African and Asian cuisines. It's a great source of fiber and vitamin B_6, and it has moderate amounts of vitamin C and potassium.

4 cups cooked chickpeas, **or** 2 (20-ounce) cans jackfruit

⅓ cup Taco Seasoning (page 32)

3 tablespoons Mexican hot sauce

8 tablespoons (1 stick) butter

½ cup water

Bibb or iceberg lettuce leaves, for serving

Sliced avocado or mango, for serving

¼ cup ranch or blue cheese dressing, for serving

GLUTEN-FREE
NUT-FREE
SOY-FREE

PREP TIME
10 minutes

COOK TIME
2 hours

TOTAL TIME
2 hours, 10 minutes

1. In a 4-quart slow cooker, stir together the chickpeas or jackfruit, taco seasoning, hot sauce, butter, and water.

2. Cover the slow cooker and cook on low heat for 2 hours.

3. Place the lettuce leaves in bowls and top with the filling, slices of avocado, and a drizzle of dressing.

Per Serving: Calories: 257; Total Fat: 15g; Sodium: 442mg; Sugars: 4g; Carbohydrates: 24g; Fiber: 7g; Protein: 8g

CHICKPEA NUGGETS *Serves 4*

Vegan and vegetarian kids don't eat chicken nuggets. One day, when I was making Falafel (page 96), I thought, gosh, the kids would probably love a hummus-only nugget that would be sort of like the falafel. Thus, the chickpea nugget was born.

2 cups Hummus
(page 46)

1 cup gluten-free breadcrumbs

2 tablespoons olive oil

Honey mustard, for serving (optional)

Ranch dip, for serving (optional)

GLUTEN-FREE
NIGHTSHADE-FREE
NUT-FREE
SOY-FREE

PREP TIME
15 minutes

COOK TIME
2 to 5 hours

TOTAL TIME
5 hours, 15 minutes

1. In a large bowl, stir together the hummus and bread crumbs. Using your hands, form the mixture into 1½-inch nuggets.

2. Pour the olive oil into a 4-quart slow cooker and swirl it around to cover the bottom of the insert. Place the nuggets into the slow cooker.

3. Cover the slow cooker and cook on high heat for 2 to 5 hours, or until the nuggets are browned.

4. Serve the nuggets with honey mustard or ranch dip (if using).

Per Serving: Calories: 317; Total Fat: 19g; Sodium: 568mg; Sugars: 0g; Carbohydrates: 29g; Fiber: 8g; Protein: 11g

CHICKPEA CARNITAS *Serves 4*

I love the smell of carnitas but, of course, I don't eat pork, so it didn't take me long to replicate the spices and aromas using chickpeas instead. This dish is so yummy you'll never have someone else make your carnitas again.

4 cups Vegetable Scrap Broth (page 14) or store-bought broth

2 cups dried chickpeas

1 onion, minced

1 tablespoon minced garlic

1 tablespoon ground cumin

2 teaspoons salt

1 teaspoon chili powder

1 teaspoon dried oregano

½ teaspoon paprika

½ cup Yogurt (page 20), store-bought plain yogurt, or sour cream (optional)

1 avocado, peeled, pitted, and diced

GLUTEN-FREE
NUT-FREE
SOY-FREE

PREP TIME
10 minutes

COOK TIME
8 hours

TOTAL TIME
8 hours, 10 minutes

1. In a 4-quart slow cooker, stir together the vegetable broth, chickpeas, onion, garlic, cumin, salt, chili powder, oregano, and paprika.

2. Cover the slow cooker and cook on low heat for 8 hours.

3. Serve with yogurt (if using) and diced avocado.

Per Serving: Calories: 470; Total Fat: 13g; Sodium: 1221mg; Sugars: 15g; Carbohydrates: 72g; Fiber: 22g; Protein: 21g

SALSA CHICKPEAS *Serves 4*

Chickpeas and salsa may sound like a simple combination but it's one that tastes really good, particularly when you use homemade Taco Seasoning (page 32) and sweet corn. Use the mixture as a taco filling or spoon it over cooked rice.

2 cups dried chickpeas

1 (15.25-ounce) can corn, undrained

1 cup salsa

¼ cup Taco Seasoning (page 32)

2 cups Vegetable Scrap Broth (page 14) or store-bought broth

Corn tortillas, for serving

Sour cream, for serving

Shredded Cheddar cheese, for serving

Diced avocado, for serving

GLUTEN-FREE
NUT-FREE
SOY-FREE

PREP TIME
15 minutes

COOK TIME
6 to 8 hours

TOTAL TIME
8 hours, 15 minutes

1. In a 4-quart slow cooker, stir together the chickpeas, corn, salsa, and taco seasoning.

2. Pour in enough broth to cover the chickpeas by 2 inches.

3. Cover the slow cooker and cook on low heat for 6 to 8 hours, or until the chickpeas are tender.

4. Serve the chickpeas over tortillas with sour cream, Cheddar cheese, and avocado, or any other desired toppings.

Per Serving: Calories: 634; Total Fat: 17g; Sodium: 216mg; Sugars: 17g; Carbohydrates: 97g; Fiber: 22g; Protein: 29g

PESTO CHICKPEAS *Serves 4*

There are almost no rules with pesto. Classic pesto uses basil and pine nuts, but those ingredients can be a little pricey and you can make a truly tasty pesto using spinach and walnuts instead.

1 cup olive oil

4 cups fresh spinach or basil leaves

½ cup walnuts

½ cup grated Parmesan cheese

1 cup cooked chickpeas (see Slow-Cooked Beans, page 15)

4 cups cooked noodles, rice, or potatoes, for serving

GLUTEN-FREE
NIGHTSHADE-FREE
SOY-FREE

PREP TIME
10 minutes

COOK TIME
4 hours, 30 minutes

TOTAL TIME
4 hours, 40 minutes

1. In a 2-quart slow cooker, stir together the olive oil, spinach, walnuts, and Parmesan cheese.

2. Cover the slow cooker and cook on low heat for 3 to 4 hours, until the spinach is cooked down. Transfer the mixture to a blender and blend until nearly smooth. Transfer the sauce back to the slow cooker.

3. Add the chickpeas, re-cover the cooker, and cook on high heat for 15 to 30 minutes, until heated through.

4. Serve over noodles, rice, or potatoes.

Per Serving: Calories: 724; Total Fat: 64g; Sodium: 157mg; Sugars: 4g; Carbohydrates: 35g; Fiber: 7g; Protein: 15g

Variation Tip: This also tastes great over paneer, Halloumi, or bread cheese, a Finnish cheese that is gaining popularity in the United States. Simply add the cheese when you would have added the chickpeas and cook as instructed.

CHICKPEAS WITH CILANTRO CHUTNEY *Serves 6*

Mr. Meaty, my husband, adores cilantro chutney. As the long-suffering meat eater of the family, I like to throw him a bone every now and then. This recipe is for him, even though the protein is chickpeas instead of chicken.

2 tablespoons olive oil

2 cups dried chickpeas

4 cups Vegetable Scrap Broth (page 14) or store-bought broth

4 cups packed fresh cilantro

2 onions, coarsely chopped

½ cup chopped roasted cashews, plus more for serving

1 jalapeño pepper, coarsely chopped

1 tablespoon ginger paste

1 tablespoon freshly squeezed lime juice

2 teaspoons light brown sugar

3 cups cooked Rice (page 17), for serving

Lime wedges, for serving

GLUTEN-FREE
SOY-FREE
VEGAN

PREP TIME
10 minutes

COOK TIME
8 hours

TOTAL TIME
8 hours, 10 minutes

1. In a 6-quart slow cooker, stir together the olive oil, chickpeas, and vegetable broth.

2. In a food processor, combine the cilantro, onions, cashews, jalapeño, ginger paste, lime juice, and brown sugar. Pulse until finely chopped, but not a paste. Transfer the mixture to the slow cooker and stir to combine.

3. Cover the slow cooker and cook on low heat for 8 hours.

4. Serve over rice with lime wedges for squeezing.

Per Serving: Calories: 507; Total Fat: 14g; Sodium: 47mg; Sugars: 14g; Carbohydrates: 80g; Fiber: 14g; Protein: 18g

CUBAN LENTIL PICADILLO *Serves 8 to 10*

Picadillo is a Cuban dish that is kind of like hash and is usually made with ground beef and raisins—and my daughter, Small Fry, loves it. My vegetarian version calls for lentils and prunes, which give it that classic sweet-savory flavor that makes this dish so wonderful. Served over rice, it makes a hearty and satisfying dinner.

6 cups Vegetable Scrap Broth (page 14) or store-bought broth

1 pound dried lentils

6 carrots, peeled and cut into coins

1 onion, chopped

1 bell pepper, any color, seeded and chopped

6 garlic cloves, minced

1 (15-ounce) can tomato sauce

½ cup pitted green olives

¼ cup chopped prunes

¼ cup ground cumin

¼ cup capers

1 tablespoon apple cider vinegar

1 tablespoon dried oregano

2 teaspoons salt

½ teaspoon freshly ground black pepper

4 cups cooked Rice (page 17), for serving

GLUTEN-FREE
SOY-FREE
VEGAN

PREP TIME
10 minutes

COOK TIME
4 hours

TOTAL TIME
4 hours, 10 minutes

1. In a 4-quart slow cooker, stir together the vegetable broth, lentils, carrots, onion, bell pepper, garlic, tomato sauce, olives, prunes, cumin, capers, vinegar, oregano, salt, and pepper.

2. Cover the slow cooker and cook on low heat for 4 hours.

3. Serve over rice.

Per Serving: Calories: 412; Total Fat: 2g; Sodium: 1124mg; Sugars: 13g; Carbohydrates: 80g; Fiber: 21g; Protein: 19g

LENTIL BOLOGNESE/
MARINARA *Serves 4*

Pasta sauces tend to evolve over time, and some are even passed down generation to generation. I developed this recipe and tweaked it over many years
before I hit on this version. The great thing about making this from scratch
is you can control the ingredients. Jarred sauce tastes great but it's high in
salt and that secret ingredient found in so many processed foods—sugar. The
recipe can be made two ways: with "meat" (lentils) like a Bolognese, and without, as a marinara. If you like your sauce really creamy, use the coconut milk,
but it's fine to leave it out.

FOR THE MARINARA

1 (28-ounce) can diced
tomatoes

4 carrots, peeled
and minced

1 small red onion,
finely chopped

5 garlic cloves, minced

½ cup red wine

½ cup coconut milk
(optional)

1 tablespoon
dried oregano

1 tablespoon
dried parsley

1 tablespoon dried basil

½ to 1 teaspoon red
pepper flakes

1 teaspoon salt

1 teaspoon freshly
ground black pepper

1 bay leaf

**FOR BOLOGNESE
(OPTIONAL)**

½ cup dried lentils

2 cups Vegetable Scrap
Broth (page 14) or
store-bought broth

GLUTEN-FREE
NUT-FREE
SOY-FREE
VEGAN

PREP TIME
15 minutes

COOK TIME
8 hours

TOTAL TIME
8 hours, 15 minutes

To make the marinara
In a 6-quart slow cooker, stir together the tomatoes,
carrots, red onion, garlic, red wine, coconut milk (if
using), oregano, parsley, basil, red pepper flakes, salt,
black pepper, and bay leaf.

To make the Bolognese (optional)

If making the Bolognese, add the lentils and vegetable broth.

To finish either version

1. Cover the slow cooker and cook on low heat for 8 hours.

2. Remove and discard the bay leaf. Using an immersion blender, purée the sauce. Or transfer it to a standard blender, in batches if needed, and purée until smooth.

3. The sauce can be refrigerated in an airtight container for up to 5 days or frozen for up to 6 months.

For Marinara Per Serving: Calories: 104; Total Fat: 1g; Sodium: 637mg; Sugars: 9g; Carbohydrates: 19g; Fiber: 5g; Protein: 3g

For Bolognese Per Serving: Calories: 189; Total Fat: 1g; Sodium: 637mg; Sugars: 10g; Carbohydrates: 33g; Fiber: 12g; Protein: 9g

LENTIL LOAF WITH BALSAMIC GLAZE *Serves 6*

Serve this beautiful lentil loaf slathered not only in balsamic glaze, but also with a steaming helping of Mushroom Gravy (page 29), English Brown Sauce (page 27), or the classic topping: Homemade Ketchup (page 30).

1 cup dried lentils

4 cups Vegetable Scrap Broth (page 14) or store-bought broth

2½ teaspoons salt, divided

1 cup gluten-free bread crumbs

1 onion, chopped

2 large carrots, peeled and chopped

1 tablespoon minced garlic

2 tablespoons butter

½ cup milk

¾ cup Homemade Ketchup (page 30), divided

2 large eggs, beaten

1 tablespoon soy sauce

2 teaspoons Dijon mustard

2 teaspoons miso paste

2 tablespoons chopped fresh parsley

1 teaspoon fresh thyme leaves

1 tablespoon balsamic vinegar

3 tablespoons dark brown sugar

Mushroom Gravy (page 29), for serving (optional)

GLUTEN-FREE
NUT-FREE

PREP TIME
20 minutes

COOK TIME
8 to 10 hours

TOTAL TIME
10 hours, 20 minutes

1. In a 4-quart slow cooker, stir together the lentils, vegetable broth, and ½ teaspoon of salt.

2. Cover the slow cooker and cook on low heat for 4 hours. Transfer to a large bowl and stir in the bread crumbs.

3. In a food processor, combine the onion, carrots, and garlic. Pulse until finely chopped.

4. In a saucepan over medium heat, melt the butter. Add the chopped vegetables and cook for a few minutes, stirring occasionally, until soft. Stir in the milk and cook for a few minutes more. Set aside to cool.

5. In a medium bowl, whisk ¼ cup of ketchup, the eggs, the soy sauce, mustard, miso paste, parsley, and thyme until blended. Add the egg mixture to the cooled vegetable mixture and stir to combine. Add the egg and vegetable mixture to the bowl with the lentils and bread crumbs, along with the remaining 2 teaspoons of salt, and stir to combine. Transfer the mixture to a glass loaf pan. Place the loaf pan into a 6-quart slow cooker.

6. In a small bowl, whisk the remaining ½ cup of ketchup, vinegar, and brown sugar. Pour the mixture over the lentil loaf.

7. Cover the slow cooker and cook on low heat for 4 to 6 hours.

8. Serve with mushroom gravy on the side (if using).

Per Serving: Calories: 286; Total Fat: 6g; Sodium: 2208mg; Sugars: 15g; Carbohydrates: 46g; Fiber: 13g; Protein: 13g

LENTIL LASAGNA *Serves 12*

Lasagna was always my mom's holiday answer when my sister and I decided to become vegetarians in the 1990s and we said no to turkey. It was fantastic because Mom made an epic cheese lasagna. This recipe is my attempt to recreate her vegetarian version with the "meat" added back, by way of lentils.

2 cups Slow-Cooked Lentils (page 16)

1 cup chopped onion

1 teaspoon minced garlic

1 (15-ounce) can diced tomatoes

1 (8-ounce) can tomato sauce

1 (6-ounce) can tomato paste

1 teaspoon Italian Seasoning (page 33)

1 teaspoon dried oregano, crushed

1 teaspoon fennel seed, crushed

¼ teaspoon white pepper

⅛ teaspoon cayenne pepper

9 lasagna noodles

2 cups ricotta or whole-milk cottage cheese

¼ cup grated Parmesan, Romano, or asiago cheese

8 ounces shredded mozzarella cheese

4 ounces shredded or sliced Swiss cheese

1 large egg, beaten

3 tablespoons chopped fresh basil

NUT-FREE
SOY-FREE

PREP TIME
25 minutes

COOK TIME
5 hours

TOTAL TIME
5 hours, 25 minutes

1. In a large bowl, stir together the cooked lentils, onion, garlic, tomatoes, tomato sauce, tomato paste, Italian seasoning, oregano, fennel, white pepper, and cayenne. Spread about one-fourth of the lentil-tomato sauce into the bottom of a 6-quart slow cooker.

2. Arrange 3 lasagna noodles in a layer on top of the sauce, breaking the noodles to fit, if needed.

3. In a medium bowl, stir together the ricotta, Parmesan cheese, mozzarella cheese, Swiss cheese, egg, and basil. Spoon one-third of the cheese mixture over the noodles.

4. Repeat the layers twice more.

5. Top with the remaining lentil-tomato sauce.

6. Cover the slow cooker and cook on low heat for 4 to 5 hours until the noodles are tender. Serve hot.

Per Serving: Calories: 351; Total Fat: 12g; Sodium: 355mg; Sugars: 4g; Carbohydrates: 41g; Fiber: 4g; Protein: 23g

LENTIL SLOPPY JOES AND SHEPHERD'S PIE *Serves 8*

Sloppy Joes and shepherd's pie are the ultimate home-cooked comfort foods. I've adapted my lentil sloppy Joes recipe to serve as the base of the shepherd's pie recipe. If you plan to make only the sloppy Joes, stop before the mash and make only the lentil mixture.

FOR THE SLOPPY JOES

1 tablespoon olive oil

3 cups Slow-Cooked Lentils (page 16)

1 large carrot, peeled and grated

1 large onion, grated

1 bell pepper, any color, seeded and grated

16 ounces frozen peas

1 cup tomato paste

½ cup red wine

¼ cup Vegetable Scrap Broth (page 14) or store-bought broth

1 tablespoon minced garlic

1 teaspoon salt

1 teaspoon ground cumin

1 teaspoon miso paste

1 teaspoon chili powder

½ teaspoon freshly ground black pepper

¼ teaspoon paprika

FOR THE SHEPHERD'S PIE

1½ pounds boiled or baked Yukon gold potatoes

¼ cup heavy (whipping) cream

¼ cup grated Parmesan cheese

3 tablespoons butter

1 teaspoon salt

½ teaspoon freshly ground black pepper

2 large egg yolks

GLUTEN-FREE
NUT-FREE

PREP TIME
20 minutes

COOK TIME
4 to 8 hours

TOTAL TIME
8 hours

To make the sloppy Joes

1. Pour the olive oil into a 4-quart slow cooker and swirl it around to coat. Add the cooked lentils, carrot, onion, bell pepper, peas, tomato paste, red wine, vegetable broth, garlic, salt, cumin, miso paste, chili powder, pepper, and paprika and stir to combine.

2. If you are making sloppy Joes only, cover the slow cooker and cook on low heat for 4 to 6 hours.

To make the shepherd's pie

1. In a large bowl, mash the potatoes. Add the heavy cream, Parmesan cheese, butter, salt, pepper, and egg yolks and stir to combine. Spread the mashed potato mixture on top of the sloppy Joes mixture.

2. Cover the slow cooker and cook on low heat for 8 hours.

For Sloppy Joes: Per Serving: Calories: 206; Total Fat: 3g; Sodium: 404mg; Sugars: 10g; Carbohydrates: 34g; Fiber: 11g; Protein: 12g

For Shepherd's Pie: Per Serving: Calories: 360; Total Fat: 12g; Sodium: 768mg; Sugars: 11g; Carbohydrates: 50g; Fiber: 13g; Protein: 15g

Banoffee Cups, page 158

6

DESSERTS

LEMON CURD   *Makes 4 cups*

Mmm . . . Lemon Curd. So sweet and tangy and bright with lemony flavor. You can use it as a topping for cheesecake, as a filling for cookies, or layered in a parfait. You can even spread it on toast for a quick snack. So make sure you keep this on hand.

8 tablespoons
(1 stick) butter

2 cups sugar

Grated zest of 5 lemons

Juice of 5 lemons

2 teaspoons
vanilla extract

4 large eggs

GLUTEN-FREE
NIGHTSHADE-FREE
NUT-FREE
SOY-FREE

PREP TIME
20 minutes

COOK TIME
6 hours, 20 minutes

TOTAL TIME
6 hours, 40 minutes

1. In a saucepan over medium heat, stir together the butter, sugar, lemon zest, lemon juice, and vanilla. Cook, stirring, until the butter melts and the sugar dissolves.

2. Transfer the mixture to a heatproof bowl that will fit inside your 4- to 6-quart slow cooker and let cool for a few minutes.

3. In a small bowl, whisk the eggs. Add the eggs to the lemon mixture and whisk to combine. Cover the bowl with aluminum foil and put it into the slow cooker. Pour water into the slow cooker until it comes halfway up the sides of the bowl.

4. Cover the slow cooker and cook on low heat for 4 to 6 hours.

5. Let the curd cool to room temperature.

6. The curd can be refrigerated in an airtight container for up to 1 month or frozen for up to 6 months.

Per Serving (¼ cup): Calories: 165; Total Fat: 7g; Sodium: 59mg; Sugars: 26g; Carbohydrates: 26g; Fiber: 0g; Protein: 2g

LEMON CHEESECAKE FRUIT DIP *Makes 3 cups*

This dip is like eating lemon meringue pie and cheesecake at the same time. Cut up slices of your favorite fruits for dipping, along with arrowroot cookies.

8 ounces cream cheese, at room temperature

1 cup powdered sugar

1¼ cups Lemon Curd (page 146)

¾ cup Yogurt (page 20) or store-bought plain yogurt

Arrowroot cookies, strawberries, and other fruit, for dipping

GLUTEN-FREE
NIGHTSHADE-FREE
NUT-FREE
SOY-FREE

PREP TIME
15 minutes

TOTAL TIME
15 minutes

1. In the bowl of a stand mixer fitted with the paddle attachment, or in a large bowl and using a handheld electric mixer, mix together the cream cheese, powdered sugar, lemon curd, and yogurt until smooth. Transfer the mixture to a bowl.

2. Serve the dip with cookies, strawberries, or other fruit for dipping.

Per Serving (¼ cup): Calories: 183; Total Fat: 10g; Sodium: 88mg; Sugars: 22g; Carbohydrates: 22g; Fiber: 0g; Protein: 3g

APPLE PIE OATMEAL *Serves 8*

My girls love oatmeal for breakfast. This version tastes like apple pie filling and the crust mixed together (without the gluten). It's a great Christmas morning breakfast: Start the slow cooker the night before and wake up to a hot breakfast and a sweet-smelling home.

3 tablespoons butter, cut into small cubes, divided

4 unpeeled apples, cored and diced

¾ cup packed light brown sugar

1½ tablespoons ground cinnamon

½ teaspoon ground nutmeg

¼ teaspoon ground ginger

¼ teaspoon ground cloves

2 cups rolled oats (if you use old-fashioned oats, reduce the cooking time a few minutes to prevent them becoming mushy)

3 cups water

1 cup heavy (whipping) cream or coconut milk

GLUTEN-FREE
NIGHTSHADE-FREE
NUT-FREE
SOY-FREE

PREP TIME
15 minutes

COOK TIME
6 to 8 hours

TOTAL TIME
6 to 8 hours, 15 minutes

1. Spread about 1 tablespoon of the butter over the bottom and sides of a 4-quart slow cooker.

2. Scatter the remaining 2 tablespoons of butter in the slow cooker.

3. Add the apples and sprinkle them with the brown sugar, cinnamon, nutmeg, ginger, and cloves.

4. Top with the oatmeal. Do not stir.

5. Carefully, pour in the water and heavy cream

6. Cover the slow cooker and cook on low heat for 6 to 8 hours.

Per Serving: Calories: 296; Total Fat: 13g; Sodium: 41mg; Sugars: 26g; Carbohydrates: 45g; Fiber: 6g; Protein: 4g

PINEAPPLE-COCONUT QUINOA *Serves 8*

I fell for fruity breakfast quinoa at a little bistro in Salt Lake City one summer. This tropical version is one of my all-time favorites and it's so easy! It's like a piña colada but, you know, good for you.

3¾ cups coconut milk

1 cup quinoa, rinsed well and drained

1 cup pineapple chunks

2 bananas, cut into slices

¾ cup coconut flakes

½ teaspoon vanilla extract

¼ teaspoon salt

GLUTEN-FREE
NIGHTSHADE-FREE
NUT-FREE
SOY-FREE
VEGAN

PREP TIME
10 minutes

COOK TIME
6 to 8 hours

TOTAL TIME
8 hours, 10 minutes

1. In a 4-quart slow cooker, stir together the coconut milk, quinoa, pineapple, banana, coconut, vanilla, and salt.

2. Cover the slow cooker and cook on low heat for 6 to 8 hours. Serve warm.

Per Serving: Calories: 401; Total Fat: 31g; Sodium: 94mg; Sugars: 10g; Carbohydrates: 31g; Fiber: 6g; Protein: 6g

HONEY-WALNUT QUINOA *Serves 8*

This dish is incredibly simple and delicious. I threw it together on the fly and have made it several times since that happy discovery.

3¾ cups coconut milk

1 cup quinoa, rinsed well and drained

½ cup chopped walnuts

2 to 3 tablespoons honey or maple syrup

1 tablespoon ground cinnamon

GLUTEN-FREE
NIGHTSHADE-FREE
SOY-FREE

PREP TIME
10 minutes

COOK TIME
6 to 8 hours

TOTAL TIME
8 hours, 10 minutes

1. In a 4-quart slow cooker, stir together the coconut milk, quinoa, walnuts, honey, and cinnamon.

2. Cover the slow cooker and cook on low heat for 6 to 8 hours.

Per Serving: Calories: 412; Total Fat: 33g; Sodium: 18mg; Sugars: 10g; Carbohydrates: 28g; Fiber: 5g; Protein: 7g

AUNT ANNIE'S RICE PUDDING *Serves 8*

My grandpa's sister made amazing rice pudding. Alas, she also never followed a recipe. Luckily enough, I followed along pretty well and managed to guess the amounts of the ingredients. I've adapted it to cook in a slow cooker from the original stovetop version, but it's just as delicious. This is a classic rice pudding using cinnamon and raisins, but feel free to experiment with different spices or dried fruits that you enjoy.

1 tablespoon butter

6 cups milk or coconut milk

1 cup medium-grain rice

½ cup sugar

⅓ cup raisins or other dried fruit

1 tablespoon ground cinnamon, plus more as needed

2 teaspoons vanilla extract

GLUTEN-FREE
NIGHTSHADE-FREE
NUT-FREE
SOY-FREE

PREP TIME
10 minutes

COOK TIME
3 to 4 hours

TOTAL TIME
4 hours, 10 minutes

1. Coat a 4-quart slow cooker insert with the butter.

2. In the prepared cooker, stir together the milk, rice, sugar, raisins, cinnamon, and vanilla.

3. Cover the slow cooker and cook on low heat for 3 to 4 hours, or until the rice is tender.

4. Serve warm or cold. Top with a few shakes of ground cinnamon before serving, if desired.

Per Serving: Calories: 259; Total Fat: 5g; Sodium: 99mg; Sugars: 25g; Carbohydrates: 46g; Fiber: 1g; Protein: 8g

Variation Tip: Add 6 cardamom pods to the recipe for a different flavor profile for this classic. Remove and discard the pods once the pudding is cooked. Top with ground cardamom before serving, in addition to the ground cinnamon in the original recipe.

PULUT HITAM *Serves 8*

Pulut hitam is a Malaysian sticky black rice pudding made with coconut milk. We first tried this at one of our favorite restaurants and, I'll admit it, I was a little scared to make this dish on my own. I didn't want to besmirch this dessert's name. But when Mr. Meaty said, "What's the worst that can happen? We'll compost it and try again," I decided to take the risk. In the end, it was so easy to make that I found myself wishing I'd tried it sooner. You should be able to find black rice at your grocery store or at an Asian market.

8 cups boiling water

1 cup black rice

⅔ cup maple syrup

1 (13.5-ounce) can coconut milk

GLUTEN-FREE
NIGHTSHADE-FREE
NUT-FREE
SOY-FREE
VEGAN

PREP TIME
10 minutes

COOK TIME
3 hours

TOTAL TIME
3 hours, 10 minutes

1. In a 4-quart slow cooker, stir together the boiling water, black rice, and maple syrup.

2. Cover the slow cooker and cook on low heat for 3 hours.

3. Serve in bowls topped with coconut milk.

Per Serving: Calories: 265; Total Fat: 12g; Sodium: 10mg; Sugars: 17g; Carbohydrates: 38g; Fiber: 2g; Protein: 3g

BLUEBERRY POLENTA CAKE *Serves 12*

I created this cake on a bit of a whim when I needed something for a work function. It's sort of like a sweet cornbread and, with the honey-lemon glaze, I have to admit, I'm a little bit in love with it.

FOR THE POLENTA CAKE

1 cup (2 sticks) butter, at room temperature, plus more for greasing

¾ cup gluten-free flour

¾ cup polenta

1½ teaspoons baking powder

1 teaspoon salt

¼ teaspoon baking soda

¾ cup granulated sugar

1 teaspoon vanilla extract

2 large eggs

1 cup Yogurt (page 20) or store-bought plain yogurt

1 cup fresh blueberries

FOR THE GLAZE (OPTIONAL)

4 tablespoons butter

¼ cup honey or maple syrup

¼ cup powdered sugar

1 tablespoon freshly squeezed lemon juice

GLUTEN-FREE
NIGHTSHADE-FREE
NUT-FREE
SOY-FREE

PREP TIME
10 minutes

COOK TIME
4 hours

TOTAL TIME
4 hours, 10 minutes

To make the polenta cake

1. Coat a baking dish that will fit inside a 6-quart slow cooker with butter.

2. In a large bowl, whisk the flour, polenta, baking powder, salt, and baking soda. Set aside.

3. In the bowl of a stand mixer fitted with the paddle attachment, or in a large bowl and using a hand-held electric mixer, beat the butter, granulated sugar, and vanilla for 3 to 5 minutes, until pale and fluffy.

4. One at a time, beat in the eggs until well mixed. Add half the flour mixture and half the yogurt and beat to combine. Add the remaining flour mixture and yogurt and beat until combined.

Continued

5. Using a spoon, gently stir in the blueberries.

6. Using a spatula, spread the batter into the prepared baking dish and smooth the top. Place the baking dish into the slow cooker. Carefully pour water into the slow cooker until it reaches about halfway up the sides of the baking dish.

7. Cover the slow cooker and cook on low heat for 4 hours, rotating the baking dish halfway through the cooking time for even baking.

8. Remove the baking dish from the slow cooker and let cool.

To make the glaze (if using)

In a saucepan over medium heat, combine the butter, honey, powdered sugar, and lemon juice. Cook, stirring, until smooth. Drizzle the glaze over the top of the cake.

Per Serving: Calories: 255; Total Fat: 17g; Sodium: 350mg; Sugars: 15g; Carbohydrates: 24g; Fiber: 2g; Protein: 3g

BLUEBERRY-LEMON
BREAD PUDDING *Serves 6 to 8*

This is my go-to potluck dessert because I can pull the bread scraps out of the freezer and throw it together with little or no notice. It's always a big hit. Whenever the bread in our house gets stale, I just cut it in cubes, put the cubes in a freezer bag, and toss the bag in the freezer.

1 tablespoon butter

2 cups fresh blueberries

Grated zest of 1 lemon

1 cup heavy (whipping) cream

1 cup milk

5 tablespoons granulated sugar

4 large eggs

1 teaspoon vanilla extract

3 cups gluten-free bread cubes (from about 6 slices)

Powdered sugar, for dusting

GLUTEN-FREE
NIGHTSHADE-FREE
NUT-FREE
SOY-FREE

PREP TIME
2 hours, 15 minutes

COOK TIME
4 hours

TOTAL TIME
6 hours, 15 minutes

Variation Tip: You can make this bread pudding with just about any berry or dried fruit. One of my favorite variations is orange zest and cranberries.

1. Coat a 1-quart baking dish with butter.

2. In the prepared baking dish, stir together the blueberries and lemon zest. Place the baking dish into a 6-quart slow cooker.

3. In a large measuring cup with a spout, whisk the heavy cream, milk, granulated sugar, eggs, and vanilla. Pour the egg mixture over the blueberries.

4. Press the bread cubes down into the liquid in the baking dish and let stand for 2 hours.

5. Carefully pour water into the slow cooker until it reaches about halfway up the sides of the baking dish.

6. Cover the slow cooker and cook on low heat for 4 hours.

7. Remove the baking dish from the slow cooker and let cool. Dust the bread pudding with powdered sugar and serve hot or cold.

Per Serving: Calories: 359; Total Fat: 23g; Sodium: 244mg; Sugars: 21g; Carbohydrates: 34g; Fiber: 2g; Protein: 7g

STICKY TOFFEE BREAD PUDDING *Serves 6 to 8*

We fell completely in love with sticky toffee pudding during one of our summer vacations in England. I'm not a huge baker, but Sticky Toffee Bread Pudding in a slow cooker? That I can pull off pretty easily! Give it a shot—it's simple and delicious.

FOR THE BREAD PUDDING

1 tablespoon butter

2 cups diced apricot

1 cup heavy (whipping) cream

1 cup milk

5 tablespoons light brown sugar

4 large eggs

2 rounded teaspoons instant espresso powder

1 teaspoon vanilla extract

1 teaspoon ground cinnamon

½ teaspoon ground nutmeg

3 cups gluten-free bread cubes (from about 6 slices)

FOR THE SAUCE

8 tablespoons (1 stick) butter

¾ cup packed dark brown sugar

½ cup heavy (whipping) cream

2 teaspoons vanilla extract

½ cup chopped pecans, toasted (optional)

GLUTEN-FREE
NIGHTSHADE-FREE
SOY-FREE

PREP TIME
2 hours, 15 minutes

COOK TIME
4 hours

TOTAL TIME
6 hours, 15 minutes

To make the bread pudding

1. Coat a 1-quart baking dish with butter and add the apricots to the dish. Place the baking dish into a 6-quart slow cooker.

2. In a large measuring cup with a spout, whisk the heavy cream, milk, brown sugar, eggs, espresso powder, vanilla, cinnamon, and nutmeg. Pour the egg mixture over the apricots.

3. Press the bread cubes down into the liquid in the baking dish and let stand at room temperature for 2 hours.

4. Carefully pour water into the slow cooker until it reaches about halfway up the sides of the baking dish.

5. Cover the slow cooker and cook on low heat for 4 hours. Serve warm or chilled.

To make the sauce

1. In a saucepan over low heat, melt the butter.

2. Add the brown sugar and heavy cream and cook, stirring occasionally, for 3 to 4 minutes. Stir in the vanilla.

3. Pour about half the toffee sauce over the bread pudding and reserve the rest.

4. Stir the pecans (if using) into reserved toffee sauce and serve it on the side.

Per Serving: Calories: 487; Total Fat: 35g; Sodium: 354mg; Sugars: 24g; Carbohydrates: 39g; Fiber: 2g; Protein: 7g

BANOFFEE CUPS *Serves 12*

Another English treat we fell for is perhaps the sweetest dessert I actually enjoy. It's called banoffee, and it's a combination of banana, toffee, and coffee. I make this version in a slow cooker with a can of condensed milk, an almond butter cookie, caramelized bananas, and the tastiest whipped cream you'll ever make. This is probably the least healthy dessert I make, but it sure is tasty. You'll need 12 (3-ounce) ramekins for serving this dessert.

FOR THE TOFFEE

1 (14-ounce) can sweetened condensed milk

FOR THE ALMOND BUTTER COOKIES

1 cup almond butter

2 large eggs

FOR THE CARAMELIZED BANANAS

4 bananas

½ cup packed light brown sugar

FOR THE COFFEE WHIPPED CREAM

½ cup heavy (whipping) cream

1 tablespoon powdered sugar

½ teaspoon instant coffee

GLUTEN-FREE
NIGHTSHADE-FREE
SOY-FREE

PREP TIME
8 hours

COOK TIME
9 hours

TOTAL TIME
17 hours

To make the toffee

1. Place a clean kitchen towel in the bottom of a slow cooker. Place the unopened can of condensed milk on top of the towel.

2. Fill the slow cooker with water to cover the can, cover the slow cooker, and cook on low heat for 8 hours.

3. Remove and refrigerate the can for 8 hours or overnight.

To make the almond butter cookies

1. Line a baking sheet with parchment paper.

2. In a large bowl, whisk the almond butter and eggs until smooth. Drop heaping teaspoons of the mixture onto the prepared baking sheet. Place the sheet in the freezer for about 1 hour.

3. Preheat the oven to 350°F.

4. Remove the baking sheet from the freezer and lightly press the cookie dough with a fork in two directions to make a checkerboard pattern.

5. Bake for 5 to 10 minutes until the edges are crisp and the centers still soft. Let cool.

To make the caramelized bananas

In a skillet over medium heat, stir together the bananas and brown sugar. Cook for about 2 minutes per side, stirring frequently, until slightly caramelized.

To make the coffee whipped cream

In a medium bowl, combine the heavy cream, powdered sugar, and instant coffee. Using a handheld electric mixer, whip the cream until stiff peaks form.

To assemble the banoffee cups

1. Open the can of chilled condensed milk and spread a layer in each serving ramekin.

2. Top with a layer of caramelized bananas, a layer of coffee whipped cream, and an almond butter cookie.

Per Serving: Calories: 214; Total Fat: 8g; Sodium: 58mg; Sugars: 30g; Carbohydrates: 34g; Fiber: 1g; Protein: 5g

FRUIT CRISP *Serves 12*

Fruit Crisp is my go-to seasonal dessert. It's a fantastic dessert to make with whatever fruit you find at the farmers' market. Stone fruit? Check. Berries? Check. Mix 'em up? Check. The fruits may vary, but the taste is always delicious.

9 tablespoons (1 stick plus 1 tablespoon) butter, at room temperature, divided

6 cups diced fresh fruit (apples, pears, peaches, blueberries, strawberries, rhubarb, or a mix of what's in season)

⅔ cup granulated sugar

⅔ cup oatmeal of choice

⅔ cup packed light brown sugar

½ cup gluten-free flour

2 teaspoons ground cinnamon

1 teaspoon ground nutmeg

½ cup chopped toasted pecans

GLUTEN-FREE
NIGHTSHADE-FREE
SOY-FREE

PREP TIME
15 minutes

COOK TIME
2 to 3 hours

TOTAL TIME
3 hours, 15 minutes

1. Coat a 4-quart slow cooker with 1 tablespoon of butter. Add the fruit and granulated sugar and stir to combine.

2. In a medium bowl, stir together the oatmeal, brown sugar, flour, cinnamon, nutmeg, remaining ½ cup (1 stick) of butter, and the pecans. Spoon the mixture evenly over the fruit.

3. Wrap the lid of the slow cooker in a clean kitchen towel, place it on the slow cooker leaving the lid slightly ajar, and cook on low heat for 2 to 3 hours.

Substitution Tip: Speed up the prep time of this tasty treat by topping the crisp with your favorite pre-made granola in lieu of the oats and nut mixture.

Per Serving: Calories: 266; Total Fat: 13g; Sodium: 65mg; Sugars: 31g; Carbohydrates: 40g; Fiber: 4g; Protein: 2g

CRANBERRY POACHED PEARS *Serves 4*

Cranberry Poached Pears are fresh and spicy and great for all ages. We first added this beauty to the dessert rotation when our youngest was less than a year old and we're still eating it because I love it so much. Adding the star anise was a bit of a gamble—I wasn't sure how the licorice flavor would taste in this recipe. It's awesome.

4 Anjou pears, cored

2 cups cranberry juice or red wine

4 star anise

4 cinnamon sticks

4 whole cloves

4 whole nutmeg

½ cup sugar

GLUTEN-FREE
NIGHTSHADE-FREE
NUT-FREE
SOY-FREE
VEGAN

PREP TIME
10 minutes

COOK TIME
4 hours

TOTAL TIME
4 hours, 10 minutes

1. In a 2-quart slow cooker, combine the pears, cranberry juice, star anise, cinnamon sticks, cloves, nutmeg, and sugar.

2. Cover the slow cooker and cook on low heat for 4 hours.

3. Transfer the pears to plates. Strain the sauce to remove the spices and serve the sauce with the pears.

Per Serving: Calories: 245; Total Fat: 0g; Sodium: 3mg; Sugars: 47g; Carbohydrates: 62g; Fiber: 9g; Protein: 1g

PUMPKIN-WALNUT BREAD *Serves 16*

This bread is made moist with coconut milk. Try it with or without the walnuts; both versions are delicious.

1 tablespoon coconut oil

3½ cups gluten-free flour

2 teaspoons baking soda

2 teaspoons ground cinnamon

1 teaspoon salt

1 teaspoon ground nutmeg

⅛ teaspoon ground ginger

2 cups packed light brown sugar

2 cups pumpkin purée

1 (13.5-ounce) can coconut milk

⅓ cup applesauce

2 cups chopped walnuts

GLUTEN-FREE
NIGHTSHADE-FREE
SOY-FREE

PREP TIME
15 minutes

COOK TIME
3 to 4 hours

TOTAL TIME
4 hours, 15 minutes

1. Coat a 1-quart baking dish with coconut oil.

2. In a large bowl, whisk the flour, baking soda, cinnamon, salt, nutmeg, and ginger. Set aside.

3. In another large bowl, stir together the brown sugar, pumpkin, coconut milk, and applesauce.

4. Add the dry ingredients to the wet ingredients and stir until combined. Fold in the walnuts. Pour the mixture into the prepared baking dish. Place the baking dish into the slow cooker.

5. Wrap the lid of the slow cooker in a clean kitchen towel, place it on the slow cooker, and cook on high heat for 3 to 4 hours, or until a toothpick inserted into the center comes out clean.

Per Serving: Calories: 331; Total Fat: 16g; Sodium: 321mg; Sugars: 20g; Carbohydrates: 45g; Fiber: 5g; Protein: 6g

BANANA BREAD *Serves 8*

Ah, Banana Bread, home of all lost bananas who find their way to my freezer after they've been forgotten on my shelf or in my fruit basket. Thankfully, you are delicious, Banana Bread.

1 tablespoon butter

1½ cups gluten-free flour

1 cup oatmeal of choice

⅓ cup honey

1 teaspoon baking soda

⅛ teaspoon salt

1 large egg, slightly beaten

3 bananas, mashed

¾ cup Yogurt (page 20) or store-bought plain yogurt

⅓ cup applesauce

½ cup chopped walnuts (optional)

1 teaspoon ground cinnamon

½ teaspoon ground nutmeg

¼ teaspoon ground ginger

¼ teaspoon ground cloves

GLUTEN-FREE
NIGHTSHADE-FREE
SOY-FREE

PREP TIME
15 minutes

COOK TIME
3 hours

TOTAL TIME
3 hours, 15 minutes

1. Coat a 1-quart baking dish with butter.

2. In a large bowl, stir together the flour, oatmeal, honey, baking soda, salt, egg, bananas, yogurt, applesauce, walnuts, cinnamon, nutmeg, ginger, and cloves. Pour the batter into the prepared baking dish. Place the baking dish into a 6-quart slow cooker.

3. Cover the slow cooker and cook on high heat for 3 hours, or until a toothpick inserted into the center comes out clean.

Per Serving: Calories: 240; Total Fat: 4g; Sodium: 224mg; Sugars: 19g; Carbohydrates: 48g; Fiber: 5g; Protein: 6g

PUMPKIN OR SWEET POTATO CUSTARD CUPS *Serves 12*

This is pretty much pumpkin pie without the crust or the processed sugar, so it's relatively guilt-free compared to other desserts.

1 (29-ounce) can pumpkin purée or sweet potato purée

1 (15-ounce) can coconut milk

1 cup maple syrup

4 large eggs

1 tablespoon Pumpkin Pie Spice (page 35)

1 teaspoon salt

½ cup packed light brown sugar

½ cup crushed pecans or walnuts (optional)

GLUTEN-FREE
NIGHTSHADE-FREE
SOY-FREE

PREP TIME
15 minutes

COOK TIME
4 to 6 hours

TOTAL TIME
6 hours, 15 minutes

1. In the bowl of a stand mixer fitted with the paddle attachment, or in a large bowl and using a hand-held electric mixer, mix together the pumpkin, coconut milk, maple syrup, eggs, pumpkin pie spice, and salt. Pour the mixture into 12 (6-ounce) ramekins. Top the ramekins with the brown sugar and pecans (if using).

2. Place 6 ramekins inside the slow cooker. Place a pan or a sheet of aluminum foil over those rame-kins and place the remaining 6 ramekins on top.

3. Cover the slow cooker and cook on low heat for 4 to 6 hours, or until the custard is set and a knife inserted into the custard comes out clean.

Per Serving: Calories: 219; Total Fat: 10g; Sodium: 227mg; Sugars: 25g; Carbohydrates: 32g; Fiber: 3g; Protein: 4g

(PUMPKIN SPICE) CHEESECAKE *Serves 8*

Slow cooker cheesecake is so easy. You can make this one in a delicious creamy vanilla flavor or swirl in some Pumpkin Spice Latte Syrup (page 36) to transform it into pumpkin spice cheesecake. Either way, it's irresistible.

FOR THE CRUST

1 cup crushed pecans

2 tablespoons light brown sugar

3 tablespoons melted butter

FOR THE FILLING

16 ounces cream cheese, at room temperature

¾ cup sugar

2 large eggs, at room temperature

¼ cup heavy (whipping) cream

2 teaspoons vanilla extract

1 tablespoon gluten-free flour

¼ cup Pumpkin Spice Latte Syrup (page 36; optional)

GLUTEN-FREE
NIGHTSHADE-FREE
SOY-FREE

PREP TIME
15 minutes, plus
3 hours cooling

COOK TIME
3 hours

TOTAL TIME
6 hours, 15 minutes

To make the crust

In a medium bowl, stir together the pecans, brown sugar, and melted butter. Press the mixture into a 1-quart baking dish. Set aside.

To make the filling

1. In the bowl of a stand mixer fitted with the paddle attachment, or in a large bowl and using a hand-held electric mixer, beat together the cream cheese, sugar, eggs, heavy cream, vanilla, and flour until smooth. Pour the cream cheese mixture over the crust.

2. Using a spoon, swirl in the pumpkin spice latte syrup (if using) and smooth the top. Place the baking dish into a 6-quart slow cooker.

3. Carefully pour water into the slow cooker until it reaches about halfway up the sides of the baking dish.

Continued

4. Cover the slow cooker and cook on high heat for 2 to 3 hours, until the edges are no longer shiny and are set.

5. Turn off the slow cooker and let the cheesecake cool inside the cooker for 1 hour. Transfer the cheesecake to the refrigerator and let cool for at least 2 hours more before serving.

Per Serving: Calories: 457; Total Fat: 38g; Sodium: 217mg; Sugars: 22g; Carbohydrates: 25g; Fiber: 2g; Protein: 7g

KEY LIME CHEESECAKE *Serves 8*

Cheesecake with a little key lime juice is one of the best flavor combinations. Yes, please, I'll have some.

FOR THE CRUST

1 cup crushed Almond Butter Cookies (see Banoffee Cups, page 158)

3 tablespoons melted butter

FOR THE FILLING

16 ounces cream cheese, at room temperature

¾ cup sugar

2 large eggs, at room temperature

¼ cup whole milk

¼ to ½ cup freshly squeezed key lime juice

1 tablespoon gluten-free flour

GLUTEN-FREE
NIGHTSHADE-FREE
SOY-FREE

PREP TIME
15 minutes, plus 3 hours cooling

COOK TIME
3 hours

TOTAL TIME
6 hours, 15 minutes

Per Serving: Calories: 467; Total Fat: 29g; Sodium: 215mg; Sugars: 27g; Carbohydrates: 47g; Fiber: 2g; Protein: 8g

To make the crust

In a medium bowl, stir together the cookie crumbs and melted butter. Press the mixture into the bottom of a 1-quart baking dish. Set aside.

To make the filling

1. In the bowl of a stand mixer fitted with the paddle attachment, or in a large bowl and using a handheld electric mixer, beat together the cream cheese, sugar, eggs, milk, key lime juice, and flour until smooth. Pour the mixture over the cookie crust. Place the baking dish into a 6-quart slow cooker.

2. Carefully pour water into the slow cooker until it reaches about halfway up the sides of the baking dish.

3. Cover the slow cooker and cook on high heat for 2 to 3 hours, until the edges are no longer shiny and are set.

4. Turn off the slow cooker and let the cheesecake cool inside it for 1 hour. Transfer the cheesecake to the refrigerator and let cool for at least 2 hours before serving.

HOW TO CARE FOR YOUR SLOW COOKER

Taking proper care of your slow cooker will ensure that you keep your favorite kitchen appliance chugging along and churning out vegetarian gems for years to come.

1. Use water or broth to cook when there is no sauce. If the recipe is relatively dry, add at least ½ cup of water or broth to the slow cooker, not only to keep the food from burning but also to keep the crock from overheating.

2. Never add cold water to a hot crock or hot water to a cold crock. The crock will crack with rapid temperature changes. Also avoid putting a hot crock directly into the refrigerator or freezer immediately after cooking. Let the crock cool first or remove the food from the crock and place it into another container.

3. Clean the crock immediately after food is cooked in it to prevent baked-on food from sticking.

4. Use only sponges rather than scouring pads to clean the surface of the crock. Likewise, use non-abrasive cleaners.

5. Never submerge the slow cooker's heating element in water. Instead, sponge clean the exterior of the slow cooker and wash the stoneware.

6. Most recipes require the slow cooker to be covered. Occasionally, however, for baking recipes to become crispy, a recipe may suggest leaving the lid ajar. Watch carefully to avoid overheating. Or, if you are unable to do so, leave the lid ajar only in the last hour or so of cooking when you can be attentive.

7. Occasionally check the stoneware for hairline cracks. While rare, they can happen and can cause your recipes to turn out poorly due to liquid and heat leaking out through the crock and onto the heating element. If discovered, retire the cracked stoneware and replace it.

8. Use the low setting as much as possible. While it can be tempting to cook not quite THAT slowly, using the low setting injects more flavor into your food and poses less risk of drying out or overcooking food and overheating your slow cooker.

9. Yes, it's dishwasher safe. Go ahead, put the stoneware insert into the dishwasher and save yourself a little elbow grease.

10. To deep clean the stoneware, fill the crock with water about two-thirds full, add 1 cup of vinegar, and 1 cup of baking soda. Cover the slow cooker and cook on low heat for 1 hour. Use a soft sponge to scrub the inside of the crock. Let the crock cool and wash it with warm soapy water. Rinse and let dry.

MEASUREMENT CONVERSIONS

	US STANDARD	US STANDARD (OUNCES)	METRIC (APPROXIMATE)
VOLUME EQUIVALENTS (LIQUID)	2 tablespoons	1 fl. oz.	30 mL
	¼ cup	2 fl. oz.	60 mL
	½ cup	4 fl. oz.	120 mL
	1 cup	8 fl. oz.	240 mL
	1½ cups	12 fl. oz.	355 mL
	2 cups or 1 pint	16 fl. oz.	475 mL
	4 cups or 1 quart	32 fl. oz.	1 L
	1 gallon	128 fl. oz.	4 L
VOLUME EQUIVALENTS (DRY)	⅛ teaspoon	——————	0.5 mL
	¼ teaspoon	——————	1 mL
	½ teaspoon	——————	2 mL
	¾ teaspoon	——————	4 mL
	1 teaspoon	——————	5 mL
	1 tablespoon	——————	15 mL
	¼ cup	——————	59 mL
	⅓ cup	——————	79 mL
	½ cup	——————	118 mL
	⅔ cup	——————	156 mL
	¾ cup	——————	177 mL
	1 cup	——————	235 mL
	2 cups or 1 pint	——————	475 mL
	3 cups	——————	700 mL
	4 cups or 1 quart	——————	1 L
	½ gallon	——————	2 L
	1 gallon	——————	4 L
WEIGHT EQUIVALENTS	½ ounce	——————	15 g
	1 ounce	——————	30 g
	2 ounces	——————	60 g
	4 ounces	——————	115 g
	8 ounces	——————	225 g
	12 ounces	——————	340 g
	16 ounces or 1 pound	——————	455 g

	FAHRENHEIT (F)	CELSIUS (C) (APPROXIMATE)
OVEN TEMPERATURES	250°F	120°F
	300°F	150°C
	325°F	180°C
	375°F	190°C
	400°F	200°C
	425°F	220°C
	450°F	230°C

SLOW COOKER SIZE CONVERSION

Most recipes in this cookbook use 4-quart and 6-quart slow cookers, whereas a few use smaller 2-quart slow cookers. If you choose only one slow cooker for purchase, a 6-quart slow cooker will suit most purposes, as you can use a smaller baking dish inside and alter the cooking time slightly for dishes suggesting smaller slow cookers.

Use the following guidelines when adapting your recipes to suit the slow cookers in your kitchen.

1. Slow cookers work best when they are about two-thirds to three-fourths full. As long as that is the case, your recipe should turn out just fine.

2. The less food there is in the slow cooker (more empty space), the quicker it will cook or burn. The more food there is in the slow cooker (less empty space), the longer it will take to cook or burn.

3. If you are using a larger slow cooker for the same amount of food, you may need less cook time. If you are using a smaller slow cooker for the same amount of food, you may need more cook time.

4. Be sure to use a baking dish if you're making a very small recipe in a larger slow cooker.

5. When using a baking dish insert, watch the slow cooker carefully and set the timer for the minimum amount of time suggested in the recipe, or even a little less, as it is much more likely to burn than a full-size recipe.

6. For most conversions of a 4-quart recipe to a 2-quart slow cooker, the easiest option may be to divide the recipe in half. Otherwise, your slow cooker might be overfilled. If your slow cooker is more than two-thirds full, you may want to increase your cook time by an hour at a time, checking it for doneness in half-hour increments.

7. For most conversions of a 4-quart recipe to a 6-quart slow cooker, you might consider increasing the recipe by 1½ or 2 times. Otherwise, you may need to reduce the cook time by one-third to half the recommended time (from 8 to 4 hours, for instance) or consider placing the recipe in a baking dish within your slow cooker. Check the slow cooker every hour to be sure your meal does not overcook.

INDEX

ABOUT THE AUTHOR

KRISTI ARNOLD is a former newspaper reporter and editor with a bachelor's in journalism and a master's in criminal justice. She lives in Georgia with her husband, "Mr. Meaty," and their two culinarily undecided children. She's a natural living enthusiast who educates friends (old and new) on frugal living and a toxin-free lifestyle.

Kristi switched to healthy "green living" after becoming a mom. She soon realized she had a lot to learn in order to make the switch and saw firsthand how overwhelming the process can be. She launched VeggieConverter.com to help with meal planning for her diverse "blended-eater" family. VeggieConverter.com transforms traditional recipe favorites into easy, organic, and (mostly) vegetarian meals that any blended-eater family can enjoy together.

Kristi developed a love of vegetarian slow cooking over the course of her family's healthy living journey. She's included many of her family-favorite recipes from the last 10 years in this cookbook for her readers to enjoy.